THE CURSED
POETS

GREEN INTEGER BOOKS
Edited by Per Bregne
København/Los Angeles

Distributed in the United States by Consortium Book
Sales and Distribution, 1045 Westgate Drive, Suite 90
Saint Paul, Minnesota 55114-1065

(323) 857-1115 / http://www.greeninteger.com
lilycat@sbcglobal.net

First Edition 2003
English language translation ©2003 by Chase Madar
First published as *Les Poètes maudits* (1888)
Back cover copy ©2003 by Green Integer

Design: Per Bregne
Typography & Cover: Trudy Fisher
Cover Photograph: Paul Verlaine

LIBRARY OF CONGRESS CATALOGING IN PUBLICATION DATA
Paul Verlaine [1844-1896]
The Cursed Poets
ISBN: 1-931243-15-8
p. cm — Green Integer 91
I. Title II. Series III. Translator

Green Integer books are published for Douglas Messerli
Printed in the United States of America on acid-free paper.

Paul Verlaine

THE CURSED
POETS

Translated from the French by Chase Madar

GREEN INTEGER
KØBENHAVN & LOS ANGELES
2003

Assembled from articles published in the journals *Lutèce* and *La Vogue*, the full version of *Les Poètes maudits* was first published in 1888. The little book helped build the reputations of the poets; it also helped fortify Verlaine's own renown, and finances.

Rimbaud, Mallarmé, and Verlaine himself don't need my introduction, but the other poets very well might. Tristan Corbière was, with Jules Laforgue, a major influence on T. S. Eliot; his directness and unfussily abrupt prosody have aged well. Marceline Desbordes-Valmore may be unknown outside of la francophonie even though Goya painted her portrait and Stefan Zweig wrote a book-length study of her. She is currently undergoing a revival of interest among French academics and deserves to be better known in the English-speaking world. Villiers de l'Isle-Adam, another virtual unknown, was the quintessential Symbolist; Edmund Wilson titled his study of the Symbolist influence in literature *Axel's Castle* in honor of Villiers' arch-symbolist drama *Axel*.

It has to be said: Much of Verlaine's prose is deep

purple fustian. A good weave, and made of sturdy stuff, yes, but still deep purple fustian. Often it's been tempting to leach out some of the purpleness, but that is not the translator's role; that would, in fact, go against the translator's humble, professional duty *not* to try and improve (read: distort) the original work.

In many instances, the poem given by Verlaine differs from the definitive version; in all cases I have taken the definitive version rather than the one originally given in *Les Poètes maudits*.

Last, I must acknowledge the help given me by previous translators: Wallace Fowlie's verse translation of Rimbaud (published by the University of Chicago Press), and Oliver Bernard's prose translation of Rimbaud (Penguin Classics) were a challenge to update and improve; both also saved me from embarrassment several times. The same goes for Val Warner's fine verse translation of Corbière, published by Dufour Editions, and for the excellent bilingual Mallarmé edited by Mary Ann Caws (New Directions). Special thanks go to the staff of New York's Alliance Française library, in particular Marie-Thérèse Casseus, and to my polyglot pal Maria Trabucchi.

— *Chase Madar*
April 26, 2000

THE CURSED POETS

Arthur Rimbaud, aged seventeen.
From a photograph by Étienne Carjat,
taken soon after meeting with Verlaine.

FOREWORD

ABOUT THE FOLLOWING PORTRAITS

The portraits we give here are completely authentic.

The one of Tristan Corbière dates back to 1875, year of the publication of his *Amours jaunes* and of his death.

We see that his demise was premature in the extreme.

We add biographically that his first name was not Tristan, but Edouard.

"Edouard" sounded good, and together with "Corbière" made a sort of croaking sound. Our own taste would have kept this echoing Christian name, very English and very Breton. But our taste was not the poet's, and is without a doubt mistaken.

Étienne Carjat photographed M. Arthur Rimbaud in October 1871. It is this excellent photograph that the reader now has in front of him, reproduced, just like the picture taken from nature of Corbière, by the process of photogravure.

Is he not the "Sublime Boy" without the atrocious failure of Chateaubriand, but not without the protestation of lips which have long been sensual, and a pair of eyes lost in very old memories rather than any dream, however precocious? A kid Casanova, but even more so a certified expert in love-affairs, doesn't he laugh with his flaring nostrils and his handsome dimpled chin; doesn't he seem to have just said, "go take a hike" to all illusions that don't owe their existence to the most irrevocable will? The proud mop of hair could only be tousled, like cushions gracefully rumpled by the elbow of some sultanesque whim. And this virile disdain for all good grooming, so useless beside the devil's own quite literal beauty!

Manet painted Mallarmé in a timeless attitude and age in spite of the cigar and lounge jacket that the great modernist was so fond of for his portraits of men, so intuitive and so refined under his good-natured dandyism. Here the poet is in some way apotheosized, *immortalized*. Would it be going too far to remember Ingres' *Cherubini*? The Muse is not visible when she blesses the genius, but she is there all the same and it is quite another muse for a different genius! And if Mallarmé had posed for Ingres, would Ingres have done better than Manet? No!

The engraved reproduction of a lovely photograph does the greatest honor to our friend Blanchet who with patient and unaffected rendering has conquered the insurmountable difficulties of this trendy photographic art — which, by the way, we will have nothing more to do with for all the money in the world.

It's now time to congratulate our cherished collaborator of Corbière and M. Rimbaud, one very aloof, as if always about to say "I'm out the door," the other with his perfect adolescence and frightening maturity.

Rarely have physiognomies been reproduced, we are not afraid to say it, by media so simple, and therefore greater and perhaps more certain, and better made than these collected here, furiously incised with an unrestrained burin.

But looking at them again, just as the verses of these dear Cursed Ones are very steadily written (for proof we need only their perfections of all kinds), even their features are calm, like bronzes from decadent Rome — but what does "decadent" really mean? — or like polychromed marble statues. So down with false romanticism! and long live the pure, stubborn (but no less amusing) line that communicates so well, through the material structure, the incompressible ideal!

There is something impassive about these strange and handsome faces — take a good look — that irrevocably validates the peerless verses one is about to read, as well as this humble but level-headed commentary.

Forgive only the commentator's mistakes. As for his enthusiasm, love it — so much the better for him; or refuse to understand it — so much the worse for you!

Voilà.

AVANT-PROPOS

We might have called them Absolute Poets to be more cautious, but, aside from the fact that caution is hardly in season these days, our title has something for the type of reader whom we hate, and, we're sure of it, something for the survivors among the All-Powerful Ones in question, for the common herd of élite readers — a rude jab of the middle finger that makes us feel better.

Absolute by imagination, absolute in expression, absolute like the *Reys netos* of the greatest centuries.

But cursed!

Judge for yourselves!

Tristan Corbière was a Breton, a sailor, and the aloof scornful type par excellence, *aes triplex*. An unobservant Catholic who believed in the devil; a sailor of neither the navy nor merchant marine, but furiously in love with the sea, on which he only sailed in stormy weather — far too spirited even on this most spirited of horses. (There are tales of his mad recklessness.) So scornful of Success and Glory that he seemed to defy this pair of idiots to provoke his pity!

Let us pass over the man who was so noble, and speak of the poet.

As a rhymer and a prosodist he was not at all flawless, which is to say, not at all tedious. Nothing among the Greats like him is flawless, starting with Homer, who sometimes sleeps, to the very human Goethe (whatever they may say), to the more than erratic Shakespeare. The flawless ones are . . . well, they are what they are: wooden, utterly wooden. But Corbière was very madly flesh and bone.

His verse lives, laughs, weeps very little, mocks well and jeers even better. Bitter and salty like his beloved Ocean, not at all soothing as his turbulent friend sometimes is, but churning like the rays of the sun, moon and stars in the phosphorescence of surging, raging waves!

He became Parisian instantly, but without the Parisian's unclean pettiness: a few hiccups, then a vomiting of irony, natty and ferocious, made of fever and bile exacerbating themselves in genius, and with such mad abandon!

RESCOUSSE

Si ma guitare
Que je répare,
Trois fois barbare,
Kriss indien,

Cric de supplice,
Bois de justice,
Boîte a malice,
Ne fait pas bien . . .

Si ma voix pire
Ne peut te dire
Mon doux martyre . . .
— Métier de chien! —

Si mon cigare,
Viatique et phare,
Point ne t'égare;
— Feu de brûler . . .

Si ma menace,
Trombe qui passe,
Manque de grâce;
— Muet de hurler! . . .

Si de mon âme
La mer en flamme
N'a pas de lame;
— Cuit de geler . . .

Vais m'en aller!

RESCUE

If my guitar which I repair, triply barbaric,
Indian *kriss*,
   Torturer's tool, guillotine, bag of tricks, doesn't
do well . . .
   If my worse voice can't tell you of my sweet
martyrdom . . . — A dog's life! —
   If my cigar, comfort and lighthouse, doesn't
bother you at all; — Fire for burning . . .
   If my menace, passing cyclone, lacks
gracefulness; — Mute from howling! . . .
   If my soul the sea in flames has no sharp edge
— Cooks by freezing . . .
   Then I'm leaving!

Before passing on to the Corbière that we like best, while adoring all the others, we must dwell on the Parisian Corbière, on the Scorner and Mocker of all and everyone, including himself.

Read again this

ÉPITAPHE

Il se tua d'ardeur, ou mourut de paresse.
S'il vit, c'est par oubli; voici ce qu'il se laisse:

— Son seul regret fut de n'être pas sa
    maîtresse. —

Il ne nacquit par aucun bout,
Fut toujours poussé vent-debout
Et fut un arlequin — ragoût,
Mélange adultère de tout.

Du *je-ne-sais-quoi.* — Mais ne sachant où;
De l'or, — mais avec pas le sou;
Des nerfs, — sans nerf. Vigueur sans force;
De l'élan, — avec une entorse;
De l'âme, — et pas de violon;
De l'amour, — mais pire étalon;
— Trop de noms pour avoir un nom. —

EPITAPH

He killed himself with fervor, or died of indolence. If he lived, it was an oversight; here is what he let himself:

— His only regret was not to be his own mistress —

He wasn't born for any end, was always blown forward by the wind and was a harlequin-stew, an adulterous mix of everything.

Of *je ne sais quoi*. — But not knowing where; of gold, — but penniless; of nerves, — but nerveless. Vigor without force; of élan, — but with a sprained ankle; of soul — and no violin; of love, — but of the lowest kind; — Too many names to have a name. —

Let us move on to lines of even greater wit.

Pas poseur, — posant pour *l'unique*;
Trop naïf étant trop cynique;
Ne croyant à rien, croyant tout.
— Son goût était dans le dégoût.

Trop *soi* pour se pouvoir souffrir,
L'esprit à sec et la tête ivre,
Fini, mais ne sachant finir,

17

Il mourut en s'attendant vivre
Et vécut, s'attendant mourir.

Ci-gît, coeur sans coeur, mal planté,
Trop réussi comme raté.

    Not a poseur, — posing as the *unique*; too
naive, being too cynical; not believing in
anything, believing all. — His taste was for
disgust.
    Too much his own to be able to suffer, the spirit
dried up and the head drunk, finished, but not
knowing how to end, he died expecting to live
and lived, expecting to die.
    Here lies, this heartless heart, poorly planted,
too successful as a failure.

As for the rest, we would have to cite the entire
section of this book, and then the entire book, or rather
it would be necessary to reprint this unique work, *Les
Amours jaunes*, which appeared in 1873 and is today
nearly impossible to find, a book in which Villon and
Pyrrho would be pleased to find an often worthy rival
— and the most renowned of today's true poets would
find a master (to say the least) of their own stature.
    But wait, we don't want to move on to Corbière the
Breton and sailor without showing a few last free-stand-

ing verses from this same section of the *Amours jaunes*.

About a friend who died "de *chic*, de boire ou de phtisie"/"of *chic*, of drink or of T.B.":

> Lui qui sifflait si haut son petit air de tête.

> He who whistled his little melody so loud.

About the same one, probably:

> Comme il était bien Lui, ce Jeune plein de sève!
> Àpre à la vie O gué! . . . et si doux en son rêve.
> Comme il portait sa tête ou la couchait
>   gaîment!

> How he was so well Himself, this Youth full of sap! Fierce for life O gué . . . and so mild in his dream. How he held his head up or lay it to sleep so gaily!

And then this rambunctious sonnet, with such a vibrant rhythm:

HEURES

> Aumône au malandrin en chasse
> Mauvais oeil à l'oeil assassin!

Fer contre fer au spadassin!
— Mon âme n'est pas en état de grâce! —

Je suis le fou de Pampelune,
J'ai peur du rire de la Lune,
Cafarde avec son crêpe noir . . .
Horreur! tout est donc sous un éteignoir.

J'entends comme un bruit de crécelle . . .
C'est la male heure qui m'appelle.
Dans le creux des nuits tombe un glas . . . deux glas.

J'ai compté plus de quatorze heures . . .
L'heure est une larme. — Tu pleures,
Mon coeur! . . . Chante encor, va! — Ne compte pas.

HOURS

Alms to the rogue on the run, the evil eye to
the murderous look! Sword against the hired
killer's sword! — My soul is not in a state of
grace! —

I am the madman of Pampelune, I'm afraid of
the moon's laughter, a sneak with his black
pall . . . Horror! All is under a candle-snuffer.

I hear something like the noise of a rattle . . .
It's the evil hour that calls me. In the hollow of
the night tolls a knell . . . two knells.

I've counted more than fourteen hours . . . An
hour is a tear. — You weep, my Heart! . . . Keep
singing, go! — Don't count.

Let us humbly admire — between parentheses —
this forceful language, simple in its charming brutal-
ity, so surprisingly proper; this strict *science* of verse;
this rhyme which is so strange, if not rich to excess.
And let us speak now of an even superior Corbière.
What a Breton bretonning in the grand old style!
The child of the moors and great oaks and riverbanks
that were! And how he remembers and cherishes, this
frightening faux-skeptic, the closely held superstitions
of his tender, rustic brethren of the coast!
Listen, or rather look; look, or rather listen (for how
to express one's sensations with this monster?) to these
fragments, taken at random, from his *Pardon de sainte
Anne*.

> Mère taillée à coups de hache,
> Tout coeur de chêne dur et bon,
> Sous l'or de ta robe se cache
> L'âme en pièce d'un franc-Breton!
>
> Vielle verte à face usée
> comme la pierre du torrent,
> Par des larmes d'amour creusée,

21

Séchée avec des pleurs de sang . . .
. . . .

— Bâton des aveugles! Béquille
Des vieilles! Bras des nouveau-nés!
Mêre de madame ta fille!
parente des abandonnés!

— O Fleur de la pucelle neuve!
Fruit de l'épouse au sein grossi,
Reposoir de la femme veuve . . .
Et du veuf Dame-de-merci!
. . . .

Prends pitié de la fille-mère,
Du petit au bord du chemin.
Si quelqu'un lui jette la pierre,
Que la pierre se change en pain!

Mother hewn by hatchet blows, all heart of
oak, hard and strong, under the gold of your dress
hides the soul in the form of a one-franc coin.
    Green old woman with a well-worn face like
the stone of the stream, hollowed by tears of love,
dried with sobs of blood . . .
. . . .
    Cane for the blind! Crutch for the old! Arm for
the new-born child! Mother of madam your
daughter! Kin to the abandoned!

22

Oh Flower of the virgin maid! Fruit of the wife
with swelling breast, the widow's altar of repose
. . . and to the widower, Lady of Mercy!
. . . .
Take pity on the unwed mother, on the child at
the side of the road. If someone should cast a
stone at him, may the stone turn into bread!

Impossible to cite all of this *Pardon* in the restricted
space we have imposed on ourselves. But it would be
wrong to take leave of Corbière without giving in full
the poem titled "The End," which holds the whole of
the sea.

LA FIN

Oh combien de marins, combiens de capitaines . . .
                                        (V. HUGO)

Eh bien, tous ces marins — matelots,
     capitaines,
Dans leur grand Océan à jamais engloutis . . .
Partis insoucieux pour leurs courses lointaines,
Sont morts — absolument comme ils étaient
     partis.

Allons! c'est leur métier; ils sont morts dans
     leur bottes!

23

Leur *boujaron* au coeur, tout vifs dans leur
   capotes . . .
— Morts . . . Merci: la *Camarde* a pas le pied
   marin;
Qu'elle couche avec vous: c'est votre bonne-
   femme . . .
— Eux, allons donc: Entiers! enlevés par la
   lame!
      Ou perdus dans un grain . . .

Un grain . . . est-ce mort, ça? la basse voilure
Battant à travers l'eau! — Ça se dit
   encombrer . . .
Un coup de mer plombé, puis la haute mâture
Fouettant les flots ras — et ça se dit *sombrer*.

— Sombrer — Sondez ce mot. Votre *mort* est
   bien pâle
Et pas grand-chose à bord, sous la lourde
   rafale . . .
Pas grand'chose devant le grand sourire amer
Du matelot qi lutte. — Allons donc, de la
   place! —
Vieux fantôme éventé, la Mort change de face:
      Le Mer! . . .

Noyés? — Eh allons donc! Les *noyés* sont d'eau
   douce.
— Coulés! corps et bien! Et jusqu'au petit
   mousse,
Le défi dans les yeux, dans les dents le juron!
À l'écume crachant une chique râlée,
Buvant sans hauts-de-coeur la *grand-tasse*
   salée . . .
      — Comme ils ont bu leur boujaron. —
. . . .

— Pas de fond de six pieds, ni rats de cimetière:
Eux ils vont aux requins! L'âme d'un matelot,
Au lieu de suinter dans vos pommes de terre,
     Respire à chaque flot.

— Voyez à l'horizon se soulever la houle;
     On dirait le ventre amoureux
D'une fille de joie en rut, à moitié soûle . . .
     Ils sont là! — La houle a du creux. —

— Écoutez, écoutez la tourmente qui
   beugle! . . .
C'est leur anniversaire. — Il revient bien
   souvent. —
O poète, gardez pour vous vos chants d'aveugle;
— Eux: le *De profundis* que leur corne le vent.

... Qu'ils roulent infinis dans les espaces
  vierges! ...
        Qu'ils roulent verts et nus,
Sans clous et sans sapin, sans couvercle, sans
  cierges ...
— Laissez-les donc rouler, *terriens* parvenus!

THE END

Oh how many sailors, how many captains ...
                                        (V. HUGO)

All right, all these sailors — ordinary seamen,
captains, in their great ocean swallowed up forever
... having left without a worry for their faraway
routes, are dead — as absolutely as they left home.

So what! That's their trade; they died in their
boots! Their *ration of rum* at heart, so lively in
their hooded coats ... — *Dead* ... No thanks:
the *Grim Reaper* doesn't have the maritime step;
let her sleep with you, she's your maidservant ...
— As for them, so what: Utterly! Taken away by
the surge! Or lost in a squall ...

A squall ... is that death? The low sails
slapping through the water! — That is called
floundering ... A blast of the leaden sea, then the

26

high mast whipping the low waves — and that is called *foundering*

Foundering — fathom this word. Your *death* is quite pale and not at all important, under the heavy storm, nothing much before the great bitter smile of the struggling sailor. — Come on now, make room! — A stale old ghost, Death changes its face: The Sea! . . .

Drowned? . . . Come on! The drowned are of fresh water. — Sunk! Bodies and belongings! Even up to the little cabin boy, defiance in their eyes, in their teeth the curse! Into the foam spitting a chewed tobacco plug, drinking down without nausea the *great salty cup* . . . Just as they drank their rationed rum. —

. . . .

No six-foot hole, no cemetery rats: There they go to the sharks! The soul of a sailor, instead of oozing from your potatoes breathes with each wave.

Look at the horizon rise above the swell; one would call it the amorous belly of a whore in heat, half-drunk . . . There they are! — The swell has its hollows. —

— Listen, listen to the bellowing storm! . . . It's their anniversary. — It comes back often. — Oh

27

poet, keep for yourself your blind man's cries; —
For them: the *De profundis* that the wind
trumpets to them.

   . . . May they roll infinitely in the virgin
spaces! . . . May they roll green and naked,
without nails and without pinewood, without
coffin-lid or candles . . . Let them roll, then,
upstart *land-lubbers*!

We have had the joy of knowing Arthur Rimbaud. Today things separate us from him without, of course, his genius and his character ever having lacked our deep admiration.

At the relatively distant time of our intimacy, Arthur Rimbaud was a boy of sixteen and seventeen, already endowed with all the poetic equipment that the real public must know about, and which we will try to analyze here while citing as much of his work as we can.

The man was tall, well-built, almost athletic, with the perfectly oval face of an exiled angel, with tousled fair chestnut hair and unnervingly blue eyes. From the Ardennes, he possessed a fine peasant accent which he lost all too quickly, the gift of speedy assimilation being native to that region's people — which could well explain the rapid exhaustion, under the pale sun of Paris, of his *Inspiration*, if we may talk like our fathers, for whom direct and proper language was not always wrong!

We will begin with the first part of Rimbaud's work, the work of his quite young adolescence, — sublime wild oats, miraculous puberty! — and then examine the varied evolutions of this impetuous spirit, until its literary end.

Here a parenthesis, and if these lines happen to fall under his eyes, then let Arthur Rimbaud know that we do not judge men's motives, and let him be assured of our complete approval of (and our dark sorrow at, as well) his abandonment of poetry, provided, as we don't doubt, that this abandonment was for him sensible, honest, and necessary.

Rimbaud's work, starting at the period of his extreme youth, that is to say 1869, '70, '71, is plentiful enough and would make a respectable volume. It is made up of generally short poems, of sonnets, triolets, poems in stanzas of four, five and six verses. The poet never uses rhyming couplets. His verse, solidly built, rarely employs elaborate conceits. Few libertine caesuras, still fewer enjambments. The choice of words is always precise, sometimes pedantic by design. The language is tight and remains clear even when the idea submerges or when the meaning obscures. Very respectable rhymes.

We don't know how to better justify what we have just said than by presenting the sonnet of the

VOYELLES

A noir, E blanc, I rouge, U vert, O bleu:
   voyelles,

Je dirai quelque jour vos naissances latentes.
A, noir corset velu des mouches éclatantes
Qui bombinent autour des puanteurs cruelles,

Golfes d'ombre; E, candeurs des vapeurs et des
    tentes,
Lances des glaciers fiers, rois blancs, frissons
    d'ombelles;
I, pourpres, sang craché, rire des lèvres belles
Dans la colère ou les ivresses pénitentes;

U, cycles, vibrements divins des mers virides,
Paix des pâtis semés d'animaux, paix des rides
Que l'alchimie imprime aux grands fronts
    studieux;

O, suprême Clairon plein de strideurs étranges,
Silences traversés des Mondes et des Anges:
— O l'Oméga, rayon violet des Ses Yeux!

Black A, white E, red I, green U, blue O:
vowels, one day I will tell of your secret births.
A, a hairy black corset of bright flies which buzz
around cruel stenches,
    Abysses of shadow; E, innocent candors of
mists and tents, lances of proud glaciers, white
kings, shivers of umbels; I, purples, spat blood,

laugh of beautiful lips in anger or in penitent
drunkenness;

U, cycles, divine vibrations of viridian seas,
peace of pastures specked with animals, peace of
wrinkles which alchemy imprints on large
studious brows;

O, supreme Clarion full of strange shrillness,
silences crossed by Worlds and by Angels: — O
the Omega, violet ray of Her Eyes!

The Muse (Oh well! Long live our fathers!), the
Muse, let us say, of M. Arthur Rimbaud, strikes all the
notes, plucks all the harp strings, strums all the guitar's
gut cords and caresses the bend of the agile bow.

Bantering and dryly comic, Arthur Rimbaud is,
when it suits him, a deadpan joker of the highest rank,
all the while remaining the great poet God made him.

A proof is the *Oraison du soir*, and these *Assis* worthy to be knelt before!

ORAISON DU SOIR

Je vis assis, tel qu'un ange aux mains d'un
     barbier,
Empoignant une chope à fortes cannelures,
L'hypogastre et le col cambrés, une Gambier

Aux dents, sous l'air gonflé d'impalpables
   voilures.

Tels que les excréments chauds d'un vieux
   colombier,
Mille Rêves en moi font de douces brûlures:
Puis par instants mon coeur triste est comme
   un aubier
Qu'ensanglante l'or jeune et sombre des
   coulures.

Puis, quand j'ai ravalé mes Rêves avec soin,
Je me tourne, ayant bu trente ou quarante
   chopes,
Et me receuille, pour lâcher l'âcre besoin:

Doux comme le Seigneur du cèdre et des
   hysopes,
Je pisse vers les cieux bruns, très haut et très
   loin,
Avec l'assentiment des grands héliotropes.

I live sitting down, like an angel in the hands
of a barber, clutching a deeply fluted mug of
draught beer, my abdomen and neck curved, a
Gambier pipe between my teeth, under the air
swelling with intangible sails.

Just like warm droppings in an old dovecote, a thousand Dreams burn gently in me: then at times my sad heart is like sapwood that bleeds the young, dark gold of its secretions.

Then, when I've carefully swallowed down my dreams, I turn myself around, having drunk thirty or forty draughts, and put myself together, to relieve the bitter need:

Sweetly like our Lord of cedars and hyssops, I piss towards the brown skies, very high and very far, with the approval of the large heliotropes.

The *Assis* have a little story which it may be necessary to tell that they be understood.

Arthur Rimbaud, who was then in his second year as a day student at the lycée de X, was an atrocious truant, and when he finally felt the need to study, tired after trekking over mountains, woods and plains for nights and days (What a walker!), he would go to the library of X and ask for books which sounded unsavory to the ears of the chief librarian whose name, not fit for posterity, dances on the tip of our pen — but what does it matter, the name of some little man with a malignant job?

This excellent bureaucrat, whose civil functions obliged him to deliver to Rimbaud, upon the latter's request, many *Tales of the Orient* and libretti of Favart, all mixed with sketchy-sounding scientific books both rare and ancient, grumbled about having to get out of his chair for this kid and sent the boy back to his unenthusiastic studies, to Cicero, to Horace, and we know not which Greeks. The boy, who already knew and appreciated his classics infinitely more than the old stinker, ended up becoming quite annoyed by all this, whence the masterpiece in question.

LES ASSIS

Noirs de loupes, grêlés, les yeux cerclés de
    bagues
Vertes, leurs doigts boulus crispés à leurs fémurs,
Le sinciput plaqué de hargnosités vagues
Comme les floraisons lépreuses des vieux murs;

Ils ont greffé dans des amours épileptiques
Leur fantasque ossature aux grands squelettes
    noirs
De leurs chaises; leurs pieds aux barreaux
    rachitiques
S'entrelacent pour les matins et pour les soirs!

Ces viellards ont toujours fait tresses ave leurs
    sièges,

Sentant les soleils vifs percaliser leurs peaux,
Ou, les yeux à la vitre où se fanent les neiges,
Tremblant du tremblement douloureux du
    crapaud.

Et les Sièges leur ont des bontés; culottée
De brun, la paille cède aux angles de leurs
    reins;
L'âme des vieux soleils s'allume, emmaillotée
Dans ces tresses d'épis où fermentaient les
    grains.

Et les Assis, genoux aux dents, verts pianistes,
Les dix doigts sous leur siège aux rumeurs de
    tambour,
S'écoutent clapoter des barcarolles tristes,
Et leurs caboches vont dans des roulis d'amour.

— Oh! ne les faites pas lever! C'est le
    naufrage . . .
Ils surgissent, grondant comme des chats giflés,
Ouvrant lentement leurs omoplates, ô rage!
Tout leur pantalon bouffe à leurs reins
    boursouflés.

Et vous les écoutez, cognant leurs têtes chauves
Aux murs sombres, plaquant et plaquant leurs
    pieds tors,

Et leurs boutons d'habit sont des prunelles
    fauves
Qui vous accrochent l'oeil du fond des
    corridors!

Puis ils ont une main invisible qui tue:
Au retour, leur regard filtre ce venin noir
Qui charge l'oeil souffrant de la chienne battue,
Et vous suez, pris dans un atroce entonnoir.

Rassis, les poings noyés dans des manchetes
    sales,
Ils songent à ceux-là qui les ont fait lever,
Et de l'aurore au soir, des grappes d'amygdales
Sous leurs mentons chétifs s'agitent à crever.

Quand l'austère sommeil a baissé leurs visières,
Ils rêvent sur leurs bras de sièges fécondés,
De vrais petits amours de chaises en lisières
Par lesquelles de fiers bureaux seront bordés.

Des fleurs d'encre crachant des pollens en
    virgules
Les bercent, le long des calices accroupis
Tels qu'au fil des glaïeuls le vol des libellules
— Et leur membre s'agace à des barbes d'épis!

Black with wens, pock-marked, their eyes circled with green rings, their pudgy fingers curled around their femurs, the fore-skulls coated with indeterminate blotches like the leprous blooms on old walls.

In epileptic fits of love they have grafted their grotesque bone-structures to the large black skeletons of their chairs; their feet intertwine with the rachitic rungs, morning and evening!

These old men have always braided themselves with their seats, feeling the sharp suns make chintzes of their hides, or, their eyes at the window where the snows fade away, trembling with the toad's dolorous tremble.

And the Seats are generous to them; worn brown, the straw yields to the angles of their backsides; the spirit of old suns lights up, swaddled in the braided ears of corn where the kernels ferment.

And the Seated Ones, knees in their teeth, green pianists, their ten fingers drumming under their chairs, listen to each other plash sad barcarolles, and their heads roll about as if making love.

— Oh! don't make them get up! That's a shipwreck . . . They spring up, growling like a slapped tomcat, slowly opening their shoulder-blades, what rage! All their pants puff out at their bloated behinds.

And you listen to them, bumping their bald heads against the dark walls, stomping and stomping their twisted feet, and their coat buttons are pupils of wild beasts which arrest your gaze from the end of the hall!

And they have an invisible hand that kills: coming back, their look filters the black venom which fills the suffering eye of the beaten bitch-hound, and you sweat, caught in a horrendous funnel.

Seated again, their thumbs sunken in dirty cuffs, they dream of the ones who have made them get up, and from dawn to dusk, clusters of tonsils under their weak chins shake fit to burst.

When austere sleep has lowered their lids, they dream of holding impregnated chairs in their arms, of darling little chairs in diapers which will be surrounded by proud desks.

Flowers of ink spitting pollen in commas rock them to sleep, along the squat calyxes, like dragonflies threading their flight among the gladiolus — and their members get aroused by the barbed ears of wheat!

We have made a point of providing all of this wisely and coolly outré poem, so reckless and so logical, up to the last verse. The reader will also have marked the forceful irony and the tremendous verve, and the poet's highest gifts remain to be considered. Supreme gifts: the magnificent testimony of Intelligence, proof both proud and French, very French, we insist on it in these days of slack internationalism, of a mystical and natural superiority of race and caste, the incontestable affirmation of that immortal royalty of the Wit, Soul and Heart of humanity: Grace and Force and Great Rhetoric annulled by our interesting, our subtle, our picturesque — but so *straight* and more than straight, stiff and uptight — Naturalists of 1883!

We have already had a specimen of Force in the few pieces cited above, but it is at this point dressed up in paradox and robust good humor such that it still appears disguised in some way. We will find it again, whole, strong and pure, at the end of this project. For the moment, it is Grace which calls us, a special grace, unknown however until here, where both the bizarre and the strange season the extreme mildness, the divine simplicity of thought and style.

For our part we know nothing in any literature so savage and so tender, so gently mocking and so affable, and with such true aim, so sonorous and magisterial, as

LES EFFARÉS

Noirs dans la neige et dans la brume,
Au grand soupirail qui s'allume,
    Leur culs en rond,

À genoux, cinq petits — misère! —
Regardent le Boulanger faire
    Le lourd pain blond.

Ils voient le fort bras blanc qui tourne
La pâte grise et qui l'enfourne
    Dans un trou clair.

Ils écoutent le bon pain cuire.
Le Boulanger au gros sourire
    Grogne un vieil air.

Ils sont blottis, pas un ne bouge,
Au souffle du soupirail rouge
    Chaud comme un sein.

Quand pour quelque médianoche,
Façonné comme une brioche
    On sort le pain,

Quand sous les poutres enfumées,
Chantent les croûtes parfumées
    Et les grillons,

Que ce trou chaud souffle la vie,
Ils ont leur âme si ravie
    Sous leurs haillons,

Ils se ressentent si bien vivre,
Les pauvres Jésus pleins de givre,
    Qu'ils sont là tous,

Collant leurs petits museaux roses
Au treillage, grognant des choses
    Entre les trous,

Tout bêtes, faisant leurs prières
Et repliés vers ces lumières
    Du ciel rouvert,

Si fort qu'ils crèvent leur culotte
Et que leur chemise tremblote
    Au vent d'hiver.

THE FRIGHTENED ONES

Black in the snow and in the fog, at the large
air-vent that lights up, their bottoms in a circle,
  On their knees, five little ones — what misery!
— watch the Baker making the heavy golden
bread.

  They see the strong white arm that turns the

grey dough and that puts it in the oven, in the bright hole.

They listen to the good bread bake. With a fat smile the Baker grunts an old tune.

They are squatting, not one of them moves, at the breath of the red vent warm like a breast.

When for some midnight meal, shaped like a brioche the bread is taken out,

When under the smoky rafters, the fragrant crusts, and the crickets, sing,

How this warm hole breathes life, so ravished are their souls under their rags,

They feel themselves to live so well, the poor Jesuses covered with frost, that they are all there,

Sticking their little pink mugs to the wire netting, mumbling things between the holes,

Quite stupid, saying their prayers and bending towards those lights of the heavens, opened again,

So hard that they split their britches and their shirts flutter in the winter wind.

What do you say to that? We, finding in another art analogies which the originality of this "little picture" forbids us to look for among all possible poets, we would say that it is reminiscent of Goya, at his best and worst. Once consulted, Goya and Murillo will no doubt prove us right.

Again from Goya *Les Chercheuses de Poux*, this time of the glowing, exasperated Goya, white on white with pink and blue effects and his special touch, singular to the point of fantastic. But how superior is the poet to the painter, by both the lofty emotion and by the singing of good rhymes!

Judge for yourself:

LES CHERCHEUSES DE POUX

Quand le front de l'enfant, plein de rouges
    tourmentes,
Implore l'essaim blanc des rêves indistincts,
Il vient près de son lit deux grandes soeurs
    charmantes
Avec de frêles doigts aux ongles argentins.

Elles assoient l'enfant devant une croisée
Grande ouverte où l'air bleu baigne un fouillis
    de fleurs,
Et dans ses lourds cheveux où tombe la rosée
Promènent leurs doigts fins, terribles et
    charmeurs.

Il écoute chanter leurs haleines craintives
Qui fleurent de longs miels végétaux et rosés,
Et qu'interrompt parfois un sifflement, salives

Reprises sur la lèvre ou désirs de baisers.

Il entend leurs cils noirs battant sous les
    silences
Pafumés; et leurs doigts électriques et doux
Font crépiter parmi ses grises indolences
Sous leurs ongles royaux la mort des petits
    poux.

Voilà que monte en lui le vin de la Paresse,
Soupir d'harmonica qui pourrait délirer;
L'enfant se sent, selon la lenteur des caresses,
Sourdre et mourir sans cesse un désir de pleurer.

THE LICE-SEEKERS

   When the child's forehead, full of red torments,
begs for the white swarm of indistinct dreams,
then two tall charming sisters come near his bed
with slender fingers which have silvery nails.
   They sit the child down before a window
casement, wide open where the blue air bathes a
bunch of flowers, and in his heavy hair where the
dew falls, there they parade their delicate fingers,
fearful and magical.
   He listens to the singing of their fearful breaths
which smell of long pinkish plant-honeys,

sometimes interrupted by a whistling sound, spittle caught on the lip or desires for kisses.

He hears his black lashes batting under the fragrant silences; and their mild, electric fingers make crackle among his grey indolences the death of small lice under their royal nails.

See how the wine of Laziness rises in him, the sigh of a harmonica that could be delirious; the child feels, according to the slowness of the caresses, endlessly arise and die an urge to weep.

There is nothing in this poem, from the rhyme's irregularity in the last stanza, to the last sentence, resting between its lack of conjunction and the final period, as if suspended and overhanging, that doesn't add to the lightness of the sketch, to the shimmer of its crosshatching, to the delicate charm of this piece. And the handsome movement, the lilting Lamartinien sway in these few verses that seems to extend into dreams and in music! It is even Racinien, we would dare to add, and why not go further and confess we find it Virgilian?

Many other examples of grace, exquisitely perverse or ravishingly chaste tempt us, but the usual limits of this second essay, already so long, makes it necessary for us to pass over so many delicate wonders and so we

will enter without more delay into the splendid em-
pire of Force where the magician invites us with his

LE BATEAU IVRE

Comme je descendais ces Fleuves impassibles, *des*
Je ne me sentis plus guidé par les haleurs:
Des Peaux-Rouges criards les avaient pris pour cibles,
Les ayant cloués nus aux poteaux de couleurs.

J'étais insoucieux de tous les équipages,
Porteur de blés flamands ou de cotons anglais.
Quand avec mes haleurs ont fini ces tapages
Les Fleuves m'ont laissé descendre où je
     voulais.

Dans les clapotements furieux des marées,
Moi, l'autre hiver, plus sourd que les cerveaux
     d'enfants,
Je courus! Et les Péninsules démarrées
N'ont pas subi tohu-bohus plus triomphants.

La tempête a béni mes éveils maritimes.
Plus léger qu'un bouchon j'ai dansé sur les flots
Qu'on appelle rouleurs éternels de victimes,
Dix nuits, sans regretter l'oeil niais des falots!

Plus douce qu'aux enfants la chair des pommes
     sûres,

47

lactescent (adj.)

L'eau verte pénétra ma coque de sapin
Et des taches de vins bleus et des vomissures
Me lava, dispersant gouvernail et grappin.

Et dès lors je me suis baigné dans le Poème
De la Mer, infusé d'astres, et lactescent,
Dévorant les azurs verts; où, flottaison blême
Et ravie, un noyé pensif parfois descend;

Où, teignant tout à coup les bleuités, délires
Et rhythmes lents sous les rutilements du jour,
Plus fortes que l'alcool, plus vastes que nos
    lyres,
Fermentent les rousseurs amères de l'amour!

Je sais les cieux crevant en éclairs, et les
    trombes,
Et les ressacs et les courants: je sais le soir,
L'Aube exalté ainsi qu'un peuple de colombes,
Et j'ai vu quelquefois ce que l'homme a cru
    voir!

J'ai vu le soleil bas, taché d'horreurs mystiques,
Illuminant de longs figements violets,
Pareils à des acteurs de drames très antiques,
Les flots roulant au loin leurs frissons de volets!

J'ai rêvé la nuit verte aux neiges éblouies,

48

Baiser montant aux yeux des mers avec lenteur,
La circulation des sèves inouïes
Et l'éveil jaune et bleu des phosphores
    chanteurs!

J'ai suivi, des mois pleins, pareille aux vacheries
Hystériques, la houle à l'assaut des récifs,
Sans songer que les pieds lumineux des Maries
Pussent forcer le mufle aux Océans poussifs;

J'ai heurté, savez-vous? d'incroyables Florides,
Mêlant aux fleurs des yeux de panthères à peaux
D'hommes, des arc-en-ciel tendus comme des
    brides,
Sous l'horizon des mers, à de glauques
    troupeaux!

J'ai vu fermenter les marais énormes, nasses
Où pourrit dans les joncs tout un Léviathan!
Des écroulements d'eaux au milieu des bonaces,
Et les lointains vers les gouffres cataractant!

Glaciers, soleils d'argent, flots nacreux, cieux
    de braises!
Èchouages hideux au fond des golfes bruns
Où les serpents géants dévorés des punaises
Choient, des arbres tordus, avec de noirs
    pafums!

J'aurais voulu montrer aux enfants ces dorades
Du flot bleu, ces poissons d'or, ces poissons
    chantants.
— Des écumes de fleurs ont bercé mes dérades
Et d'ineffables vents m'ont ailé par instants.

Parfois, martyr lassé des pôles et des zones,
La mer dont le sanglot faisait mon roulis doux
Montait vers moi ses fleurs d'ombre aux
    ventouses jaunes
Et je restais, ainsi qu'une femme à genoux . . .

Presque île, ballottant sur mes bords les
    querelles
Et les fientes d'oiseaux clabaudeurs aux yeux
    blonds.
Et je voguais, lorsqu'à travers mes liens frêles
Des noyés descendaient dormir, à reculons! . . .

Or moi, bateau perdu sous les cheveux des
    anses,
Jeté par l'ouragan dans l'éther sans oiseau,
Moi dont les Monitors et les voiliers des Hanses
N'auraient pas repêché la carcasse ivre d'eau;

Libre, fumant, monté de brumes violettes,
Moi qui trouais le ciel rougeoyant comme un
    mur

Qui porte, confiture exquise aux bons poëtes,
Des lichens de soleil et des morves d'azur;

Qui courais, taché de lunules électriques,
Planche folle, escorté des hippocampes noirs,
Quand les juillets faisaient crouler à coups de
    triques
Les cieux ultramarins aux ardents entonnoirs;

Moi qui tremblais, sentant geindre à cinquante
    lieues
Le rut de Béhémots et les Maelstroms épais,
Fileur éternel des immobilités bleus,
Je regrette l'Europe aux anciens parapets!

J'ai vu des archipels sidéraux! et des îles
Dont les cieux délirants sont ouverts au
    vogueur:
— Est-ce en ces nuits sans fonds que tu dors et
    t'exiles,
Million d'oiseaux d'or, ô future Vigueur? —

Mais, vrai, j'ai trop pleuré! Les Aubes sont
    navrantes.
Toute lune est atroce et tout soleil amer:
L'âcre amour m'a gonflé de torpeurs enivrantes.
Ô que ma quille éclate! Ô que j'aille à la mer!

(Keel)   51

Si je désire une eau d'Europe, c'est la flache
Noire et froide où vers le crépuscule embaumé
Un enfant accroupi plein de tristesses, lâche
Un bateau frêle comme un papillon de mai.

Je ne puis plus, baigné de vos langueurs, ô
    lames,
Enlever leur sillage aux porteurs de cotons,
Ni traverser l'orgueil des drapeaux et des
    flammes,
Ni nager sous les yeux horribles des pontons.

un ponton = pontoon / floating landing stage / hulk / lighter

THE DRUNKEN BOAT

As I was going down impassive Rivers, I no
longer felt guided by the haulers: whooping
Redskins had used them for targets, having nailed
them naked to the colored posts.

I was indifferent to all these crews, carrying
Flemish wheat or English cottons. When with my
haulers, these uproars having ended, the Rivers
let me float down wherever I wanted.

In the tides' furious lashing, last winter, deafer
than the brains of children, I ran! And the
unmoored Peninsulas have never undergone more
triumphant commotions.

The storm blessed my marine awakenings. Lighter than a cork I danced on the waves they call eternal rollers of victims, ten nights, without missing the stupid eye of the lanterns!

Sweeter than the flesh of tart apples to children, the green water penetrated my pinewood hull, and cleansed me of blue wine-stains and vomit splashes, scattering rudder and anchor away.

And since then I bathed myself in the Poem of the Sea, infused with stars, and lactescent, devouring the green azures; where, pale and spellbound flotsam, a pensive drowned man sometimes sinks;

Where, suddenly dyeing the bluenesses, delirium and slow rhythms under the gleams of daybreak, stronger than alcohol, vaster than our lyres, the bitter rednesses of love ferment!

I know the heavens split by lightning bolts, and the waterspouts, and the backwash and the currents: I know the evening, the dawn roused like a whole people of doves, and I have sometimes seen what man thought he saw!

I have seen the low sun, flecked with mystic horrors, lighting up with long violet congealments, like actors of most ancient dramas, the waves rolling

53

far off their shivers of venetian blinds!

I have dreamed of the green night of dazzled snows, a kiss rising slowly to the eyes of the seas, the circulation of unheard-of saps and the yellow and blue awakening of singing phosphorous!

I have followed, for months on end, the swell attacking the reefs like hysterical herds of cows, — without dreaming that the luminous feet of the Marys could force back the snout of panting Oceans;

I have collided with, do you know? unbelievable Floridas, where mingling with the flowers are eyes of panthers in human skin, rainbows stretched like bridles, under the seas' horizon, around glaucous herds!

I have seen the enormous swamps fermenting, fish-traps where a whole Leviathan rots in the rushes! Rockslides of water in the midst of the storm-lulls, and the distances cascading toward the abyss!

Glaciers, silver suns, nacreous waves, skies of embers! Hideous ships run aground at the bottom of brown gulfs where giant snakes devoured by bed lice fall from twisted trees with black odors!

I would have liked to show the children these sea bream of the blue waves, those golden fish, those singing fish. — Foams of flowers have cradled my driftings and ineffable winds have at times given me wings.

Sometimes, a martyr weary of the poles and the spaces, the sea whose sobbing caused my soft rolling, carried up to me its shadow-flowers with yellow sucker-cups and I stayed, like a woman on her knees . . .

Almost an island, tossing on my shores the quarrels and droppings of clamoring birds with pale eyes. And I sailed on, when across my frayed rigging drowned men sank to sleep, backwards! . . .

Now I, a boat lost under the hair of the coves, tossed by the hurricane into the birdless ether, I whose water-drunk carcass the Monitors and the Hanseatic vessels would not have fished out of the water;

Free, smoking, risen from the violet mists, I who pierced the reddening sky like a wall bearing — delicious jam to good poets — lichens of sunlight and azure snot;

I who ran, flecked with electric lunules, a mad plank escorted by black seahorses, when the Julys with cudgel-blows made the ultramarine skies collapse into burning funnels;

I who trembled, sensing at fifty leagues the

groans of Behemoth's rutting and the thick
Maelstroms, eternal spinner of blue immobilities,
I long for Europe with its antique parapets!

I saw sidereal archipelagos! and islands whose
delirious skies are open to the roving sailor: — Is
it in these bottomless nights that you sleep and
exile yourself, million of golden birds, oh future
Life-Force? —

But, in truth, I have wept too much! The
Dawns are heart-rending. All moons are awful, all
suns bitter: Acrid love has swollen me with
intoxicating torpors. Oh let my keel shatter! Oh
let me go out to sea!

If there is one water in Europe I want, it is the
black and cold water-ditch where into the sweet-
smelling twilight a squatting child full of sadness
releases a boat as fragile as a May butterfly.

I can no longer, bathed in your languors, O
waves, take away their wake from the cotton
steamers, nor cross the pride of banners or of
pennants, nor swim under the horrible eyes of the
hulks.

Now, what opinion is to be formulated on the
Premières Communions, a poem too long to take its
place here, especially after our excess of citations, a

poem whose wit we happen to loathe, given that it seems to stem from an unhappy meeting with a Michelet gone senile and impious, the Michelet snooping in the dirty linen of women and behind Parny (but no one adores the other Michelet more than we do), yes, what can we opine about this mammoth excerpt, other than that we love the deeply ordered design and all the verses without exception? There are some like this:

> Adonaï! Dans les terminaisons latines
> Des cieux moirés de vert baignent les Fronts
>   vermeils,
> Et, tachés du sang pur des célestes poitrines,
> De grands linges neigeux tombent sur les
>   soleils!

> Adonaï! In the Latin endings, skies streaked
> with green bathe the crimson Brows, and, flecked
> with the pure blood of heavenly breasts, great
> snowy bedsheets fall across the suns!

Paris se repeuple, written the day after the "Week of Blood," swarms with beauties.

. . . .
> Cachez les palais morts dans des niches de planches!

57

L'ancien jour effaré rafraîchit vos regards.
Voici le troupeau roux des tordeuses de
hanches!

. . . .

Quand tes pieds ont dansé si fort dans les
colères,
Paris! quand tu reçus tant de coups de couteau,
Quand tu gis, retenant dans tes prunelles claires
Un peu de la bonté du fauve renouveau, [...]

. . . .

Hide the dead palaces in nests of wood planks!
Startled, the aging daylight refreshed your looks.
Look at the red-headed flock of thigh-twisters!
. . . .
When your feet have danced so hard in anger,
Paris! when you took so many knife-blows, when
you lay down, keeping in your bright eyes a little
of the goodness of tawny renewal, [. . .]

In this order of ideas, *Les Veilleurs*, a poem which is
no longer, alas, in our possession, and which our
memory cannot manage to reconstruct, has left the
strongest impression that poetry has ever stamped upon
us. Such resonance, such breadth, such holy sadness!
And with such an accent of sublime desolation, that

in truth we dare to believe it the most beautiful thing written by Arthur Rimbaud, and by far.

Many other pieces of the highest order have passed through our hands, which malicious fortune and the whirlwind of picaresque travels have made us lose. So let us here beseech all our known and unknown friends who might possess *Les Veilleurs, Accroupissements, Les Pauvres à l'église, Les Réveilleurs de la nuit, Douaniers, Les Mains de Jeanne-Marie, Soeur de Charité* and anything else signed by this prestigious name, to be willing to send them to us for the probable case in which this work must be finished. In the name of the honor of Letters, we will repeat our prayer. The manuscripts will be religiously returned, once copies are made, to their generous owners.

It is time to dream of finishing that which has assumed such dimensions for so many excellent reasons:

The name and work of Corbière and those of Mallarmé are assured for the duration of time; some will stay on men's lips, the others in the memories of all worthy of them. Corbière and Mallarmé *have been published*, — that enormous minor detail. Rimbaud, too scornful, more scornful even than Corbière who at least flung his volume square at the century's nose, did not want any of his verse to appear in print.

One lone piece, which Rimbaud denied and disavowed, was inserted at his request, and this was done well, in the first year of the *Renaissance*, around 1873. This was called *Les Corbeaux*. The curious can regale themselves with this patriotic work, and patriotic in the good sense, a poem we heartily enjoy ourselves. We are proud to offer to those of our intelligent contemporaries a goodly portion of this rich cake of Rimbaud!

Had we consulted Rimbaud (whose address we don't know) he would have, it is probable, counseled us against undertaking the project which presently concerns us.

And so he is cursed by himself, this Cursed Poet! But the literary friendship and devotion that we will always avow to him have dictated these lines, and have made us indiscreet. So much the worse for him! But so much the better for you! All will not be lost of this forgotten treasure by its more than insouciant owner, and if it is a crime that we commit, well then, *felix culpa*!

After some stay in Paris, then divers, more or less frightful pilgrimages, Rimbaud turned around and worked (him!) in the naive style, the very and patently too simple, using nothing more than assonant rhymes, unspecific words, vulgar and childlike phrases. He accomplished in this way prodigies of tenuousness, of true haziness, of a charm almost inappreciable for being so slender and slight.

> Elle est retrouvée.
> Quoi? — L'Éternité.
> C'est la mer allée
> Avec les soleils.

> It is found again. What? — Eternity. It's the sea gone away with the suns.

But the poet was disappearing. — We mean "poet" strictly, in the rather particular sense of the word.

A surprising prose-writer followed. A manuscript whose name escapes us which contained strange mysticism and the sharpest psychological insights fell into hands which mislaid it without knowing what they were doing.

Une Saison en Enfer, which appeared in Brussels, 1873, at Poot et Cie, 37, rue aux Choux, sank with all souls on board into a monstrous oblivion, the author not having "launched" it at all. He had better things to do.

He rambled over all the Continents, all the Oceans, poorly, proudly (rich if he had wanted, from family and from social position) before having written, in prose again, a series of superb fragments, *Les Illumina-*

tions, now, we fear, lost forever.

He said in his *Saison en Enfer*: "My day is done. I'm leaving Europe. The sea air will burn my lungs, lost climates will tan my hide."

All this is very well and the man has kept his word. The man in Rimbaud is free, that is too clear and we have conceded it from the beginning, with a very legitimate reserve which we are going to accentuate in closing. Haven't we had reason, we, mad about the poet, to take him, this eagle, and hold him in this cage, under this scientific label? And could we hardly be expected (if Literature should see such a loss consummated) to refrain from ironically shouting about him, and his older (but not greater) brother Corbière, ironically? No. Melancholically? Ah yes! Furiously? Ah but yes! —:

> Elle est éteinte
> Cette huile sainte.
> Il est éteint
> Le sacristain!

> It is extinguished, this holy oil. He is snuffed out, the sexton!

STÉPHANE MALLARMÉ

In a book that will not be published, we recently wrote apropos of the *Parnasse contemporain* and its principle contributors: "Another poet and not the least of them is attached to this group. He lived then in the provinces, working as an English teacher, but corresponded frequently with Paris. He furnished the Parnasse with verses of such novelty as caused a scandal in the newspapers. Concerned, indeed! with beauty, he considered clarity a secondary grace, and as long as his verse was rhythmic, musical, strange, and when necessary, languid or excessive, he mocked everything to please those delicate souls of which he himself was the most difficult. And, as it was poorly received by Criticism, this pure poet will remain as long as there is a French language to bear witness to his colossal efforts. How he was jeered at for his 'rather affected extravagance,' as if he were some worn-out master expressing himself 'rather' indolently, as if he were some elderly poet who might have better defended himself back when he was the sharp-toothed, full-maned lion of Romanticism! In the frivolous pages at the heart of nearly all the serious Journals, it became fashionable to get a laugh by lecturing this accomplished writer about correct usage, about the true sense of beauty. Even among the most influential, there were idiots who treated him like a madman. And this is another honorable symptom: writers worthy of the name deigned to mingle with this incompetent fracas; one saw men of great wit and proud taste, masters of great common sense and just audacity act like boors — among them, alas, M. Barbey d'Aurevilly. Annoyed by the purely theoretical Impassiveness of the Parnassians, this marvelous novelist, this matchless polemicist, this essayist of genius, the uncontested first among our admired prose writers, published in the *Le Nain Jaune* a series of articles against *Le Parnasse* in which the spirit of outrage yielded only to the most exquisite cruelty; the illustrated portrait medallion consecrated to Mallarmé was particularly scabrous, so unjust that it offended each of us more than might any personal injury. But what do they matter, these errors of mere Opinion, to Stéphane Mallarmé and to those who love him as it is necessary to love him (or hate him) — immensely!" (*Voyage en France par un Français: Le Parnasse contemporain.*)

I have nothing to change in this appreciation, hardly six years old, and which could have been written the day we first read Mallarmé's verse.

From that time the poet has been able to augment his style, to do more of what he likes, — he has stayed the same, not by staying still, good Lord! but by shining with the first light of dawn, then increasing gradually to noon and then to the afternoon, as is only natural.

That is why we want, while hoping not to tire our essay's small audience, to furnish them with a sonnet and a terza rima, both early and unknown, which we believe will win them over to our dear poet and dear friend at the beginning of his talent, striking every key of his incomparable instrument.

une demande / pétition / requête

PLACET FUTILE

Princesse! à jalouser le destin d'une Hébé
Qui poind sur cette tasse au baiser de vos
    lèvres,
J'use mes feux mais n'ai rang discret que d'abbé
Et ne figurerai même nu sur le Sèvres.

Comme je ne suis pas ton bichon embarbé,
Ni la pastille ni du rouge, ni Jeux mièvres
Et que sur moi je sais ton regard clos tombé,
Blonde dont les coiffeurs divins sont des
    orfèvres!

Nommez-nous . . . toi de qui tant de ris
    framboisés

65

Se joignent en troupeau d'agneau apprivoisés
Chez tous broutant les voeux et bêlant aux
    délires,

Nommez-nous . . . pour qu'Amour ailé d'un
    évantail
M'y peigne flûte aux doigts endormant ce
    bercail,
Princesse, nommez-nous berger de vos sourires.

FUTILE PETITION

    Princess! In being jealous of the fate of a
Hebe who peeps over that cup at your lips' kiss,
I expend my ardors but have only the modest rank
of abbot and will not be depicted, even naked, on
the Sèvres porcelain.
    As I am not your bearded spaniel, nor your
lozenge nor your makeup, nor your silly little
Games and since on me I know your gaze is fallen,
O blonde whose divine coiffeurs are goldsmiths!
    Name us . . . you of whom so many raspberried
laughing smiles combine in a flock of tame sheep,
grazing on everyone's desires and bleating to
delirium,
    Name us . . . for whom Love, winged with a

fan, polishes the flute in my fingers lulling this
fold to sleep, Princess, name us the shepherd of
your smiles.

Well then, isn't this a precious hot-house flower?
Plucked, by what good fortune, by the rugged hand of
the master artisan who forged it.

LE GUIGNON = (Mauvaise chance persistante)

Au-dessus du bétail ahuri des humains
Bondissaient en clartés les sauvages crinières
Des mendieurs d'azur le pied dans nos chemins.

Un noir vent de cendre éployé pour bannières
La flagellait de froid tel jusque dans la chair,
Qu'il y creusait aussi d'irritables ornières.

Toujours avec l'espoir de rencontrer la mer,
Ils voyageaient sans pain, sans bâtons et sans
    urnes,
Mordant au citron d'or de l'ideal amer.

La plupart ont râla dans les défilés nocturnes,
S'enivrant du bonheur de voir couler son sang.
Ô mort le seul baiser aux bouches taciturnes!

Leur défaite, c'est par un ange très puissant
Debout à l'horizon dans le nu de son glaive:

(Le guignol = marionnette sans fils animée par les doigts)

Une pourpre se caille au sein reconnaissant.

Ils tètent la Douleur comme ils tétaient le Rêve
Et quand ils vont rhythmant leurs pleurs
    voluptueux
Le peuple s'agenouille et leur mère se lève.

Ceux-là sont consolés, sûrs et majestueux;
Mais traînent à leurs pas des frères qu'on bafoue,
Dérisoires martyrs de hasards tortueux.

Le sel pareil des pleurs ronge leur douce joue,
Ils mangent de la cendre avec le même amour;
Mais vulgaire ou bouffon le destin qui les roue.

Ils pouvaient exciter aussi comme un tambour
La servile pitié des races à voix ternes,
Égaux de Prométhée à qui manque un vautour!

Non. Vils et fréquantant les déserts sans
    citerne,
Ils courent sous le fouet d'un monarque rageur,
Le Guignon, dont le rire inouï les prosterne.

Amants, il saute en croupe à trois, le partageur!
Puis, le torrent franchi, vous plonge en une
    mare
Et laisse un bloc boueux du blanc couple
    nageur.

Grâce a lui, si l'un souffle à son buccin bizarre,
Des enfants nous tordront en un rire obstiné
Qui, le poing à leur cul, singeront sa fanfare.

Grâce a lui, si l'une orne à point un sein fané
Par une rose qui nubile le rallume,
De la bave luira sur son bouquet damné.

Et ce squelette nain, coiffé d'un feutre à plume
Et botté, dont l'aisselle a pour poils vrais des
    vers,
Est pour eux l'infini de la vaste amertume.

Vexés ne vont-ils pas provoquer le pervers,
Leur rapière grinçant suit le rayon de lune
Qui neige en sa carcasse et qui passe au travers.

Désolés sans l'orgueil qui sacre l'infortune,
Et tristes de venger leurs os de coups de bec,
Ils convoitent la haine, au lieu de la rancune.

Ils sont l'amusement des racleurs de rebec,
Des marmots, des putains et de la vieille
    engeance
Des loquetuex dansant quand le broc est à sec.

Les poètes bons pour l'aumône ou la
    vengeance,

Ne connaisant le mal de ces dieux effacés,
Les disent impuissants et sans intelligence.

"Ils peuvent fuir ayant de chaque exploit assez,
Comme un vierge cheval écume de tempête,
Plutôt que de partir en galops cuirassés.

"Nous soûlerons d'encens le vainqueur dans la
        fête:
Mais eux, pourquoi n'endosser pas, ces baladins
D'écarlate haillon hurlant que l'on s'arrête!"

Quand en face tous leur ont craché les dédains,
Nuls et la barbe à mots bas priant le tonnerre,
Ces héros excédés de malaises badins

Vont ridiculement se pendre au réverbère.

THE JINX

   Above the bewildered cattle of humanity were
leaping in flashes the wild manes of the beggars of
the azure, their feet in our paths.
   A black wind of ash spread out around the
banners thrashed them with a coldness
penetrating their flesh, which they hollowed with
irritable ruts.

Always with the hope of finding the sea, they traveled without bread, without sticks, without urns, biting the golden lemon of the bitter Ideal.

Most of them moaned in the nocturnal parades, getting drunk on the happiness of watching their blood flow. O death the only kiss for taciturn mouths!

Their defeat, it's by a very powerful angel standing at the horizon in the bareness of his sword. A purple congeals at the recognizing breast.

They suck at Pain as they sucked at the Dream and when they go rhyming their voluptuous sobs, the people fall to their knees and their mother rises.

The former are consoled, confident and majestic. But dragged by their footsteps are brothers who are scorned, ridiculous martyrs of tortuous chance.

Salt like wept tears gnaws at their soft cheek, they eat ash with the same love; But vulgar or buffoonish is the fate that thrashes them.

They could also arouse like a drum the servile pity of races with tarnished voices, equals of a Prometheus who lacks only a vulture!

No. Base and frequenting the deserts without

wells, they run under the whip of a raging
monarch, the Jinx, whose unheard of laugh
prostrates them.

If they have a lover, it jumps into the saddle to
make a third, the sharer! then, the torrent
crossed, plunges you into a sea and leaves a muddy
mass of the white, swimming couple.

Thanks to him, if one blows at his strange
whelk-shell, children will twist us in an obstinate
laugh, who, fists at their chests, ape the fanfare.

Thanks to him, if one scarcely decorates a
withered breast with a nubile rose that revives it,
her damned bouquets will shine with drool.

And this dwarf skeleton coiffed with a
feathered felt hat and wearing boots, whose
armpit has real worms for hairs, is for them the
infinity of vast bitterness.

Annoyed, won't they provoke the perverse,
their rapier while screeching follows the moon's
ray which snows on its carcass and escapes.

Desperate without the pride which sanctifies
the misfortune, and sad from avenging their bones
against blows of the beak, they covet hatred,
instead of grudges.

They are the amusement of they who scrape
rebecs, of brats, of whores and of the old breed of

ragged, dancing people when the ewer has run
dry.

The good poets, for alms or for revenge, not
knowing the ills of these inconspicuous Gods,
declare them impotent and without intelligence.

"They can flee having enough of each feat, like
an unbroken horse the foam of a storm, rather
than taking leave with armor-plated gallops.

"We will gorge the Conqueror with incense at
the feast: But they, why not dress these strolling
players in scarlet rags wailing for us to stop!"

When each has spat his scorn in their face,
praying under their breath for thunder, these
heroes overloaded with playful uneasiness

Ridiculously go hang themselves from the
streetlight.

From around the same period, but evidently later
rather than earlier, comes the exquisite

APPARITION

La lune s'attristait. Des séraphins en pleurs
Rêvant, l'archet aux doigts, dans le calme des
    fleurs
Vaporeuses, tiraient de mourantes violes

De blancs sanglots glissant sur l'azur des
    corolles.
— C'était le jour béni de ton premier baiser.
Mon songerie aimant à me martyriser
S'enivrait savammet du parfum de tristesse
Que même sans regret et sans déboire laisse
La cueillaison d'un Rêve au coeur qui l'a cueilli
J'errais donc, l'oeil rivé sur le pavé vieilli,
Quand, avec du soleil aux cheveux, dans la rue
Et dans le soir, tu m'es en riant apparue,
Et j'ai cru voir la fée au chapeau de clarté
Qu jadis sur mes beaux sommeils d'enfant gâté
Passait, laissant toujours de ses mains mal
    fermées
Neiger de blancs bouquets d'étoiles parfumées.

APPARITION

The moon was growing sad. Seraphim in tears,
dreaming, bow in hand, in the calm of vaporous
flowers, were drawing from dying viols white sobs
sliding down the blue of corollas. It was the
blessed day of your first kiss. My daydreaming
loving to make a martyr of me was wisely getting
drunk on the scent of sadness that even without
regret and without disappointment is left by the

74

gathering of a Dream in the heart which has gathered it. I was wandering, then, my eyes on the worn cobbles, when, the sun in your hair, in the street and in the night, you appeared to me laughing, and I believed I saw the fairy with her bright hat which once passed on my happy slumbers as a spoiled child, always letting from her half-closed hands snow down white bouquets of perfumed stars.

and the less venerable but more lovable

SAINTE   *optional accent*

A la fenêtre recélant
Le santal vieux qui se dédore
De sa viole étincelant
Jadis avec flûte ou mandore

Est la Sainte Pâle, étalant
Le livre vieux qui se déplie
Du Magnificat ruisselant
Jadis selon vêpre et complie:

A ce vitrage d'ostensoir
Que frôle une harpe par l'Ange
Formée avec son vol du soir
Pour la délicate phalange

75

Du doigt, que, sans le vieux santal
Ni le vieux livre, elle balance
Sur le plumage instrumental,
Musicienne du silence.

SAINT

At the window hiding the old sandalwood
flaking its gold paint from her shining viol
formerly with flute or mandola,
Is the pale Saint, spreading out the old book
which unfolds from the streaming Magnificat
formerly in vespers and compline:
At this monstrance stained-glass window
brushed by a harp formed by the Angel with her
evening flight for the delicate bone
Of her finger which, without the old
sandalwood nor the old book, she balances on the
instrumental plumage, musician of silence.

These heretofore unpublished poems lead us to what
we will call Mallarmé's era of celebrity. Far too few
poems of such color and music (from then on essential) appeared in the first and second *Parnasses
contemporains* where admiration can find them at its
leisure. *Les Fenêtres*, *Le Sonneur*, *Automne*, the quite
long fragment of an *Hérodiade* seem to us to be

supreme works among these supreme things, but we will not waste time by quoting from the published version, which unlike the manuscript is far from obscure, just as has happened — how? if not by THE CURSE that it has deserved — to the vertiginous book *Les Amours jaunes* by the stupefying Corbière: we would rather provide you with the joy of reading this new and valuable unpublished poem which belongs, we think, to the middle period in question.

DON DU POÈME

Je t'apporte l'enfant d'une nuit d'Idumée!
Noire, à l'aile saignante et pâle, déplumée,
Par le verre brûlé d'aromates et d'or,
Par les carreaux glacés, hélas! mornes encor,
L'aurore se jeta sur la lampe angélique,
Palmes! et quand elle a montré cette relique
A ce père essayant un sourire ennemi,
La solitude bleue et stérile a frémi.
O la berceuse avec ta fille et l'innocence
De vos pieds froids, accueille une horrible naissance:
Et ta voix rappelant viole et clavecin
Avec le doigt fané presseras-tu le sein
Par qui coule en blancheur sibylline la femme
Pour de lèvres que l'air du vierge azur affame?

GIFT OF THE POEM

I bring you the child of an Idumaean night!
Black, with a bleeding pale wing, feathers
plucked, through the glass burnt by aromatic
herbs and gold, through the icy panes, alas! still
dark, the dawn cast itself on the angelic lamp,
palms! and when she [the dawn] showed this relic
to the father trying to smile as an enemy, the blue
and sterile solitude shuddered. Oh lullaby-singer
with your daughter and the innocence of your
cold feet, welcome a horrible birth, and your
voice recalling viol and harpsichord, with your
withered finger will you press the breast through
which flows woman in sibylline whiteness for the
lips which the azure air of virgin makes hungry?

In truth, this idyll was spitefully (and *spitefully*)
printed at the end of the last regime by an irritating
weekly paper, *Le Courrier du dimanche*. But what could
this surly counter-thrust mean, given that for all men
of wit the *Don du Poème*, accused of alembicated
eccentricity, is the sublime dedication by an outstand-
ing poet to an offshoot of his own soul, born of one of
these horrible efforts that one loves even while *trying*
not to love them, and for whom one dreams of complete protection, even against oneself! —

78

The *Courrier du Dimanche* was liberal-republican and Protestant, but whether radical republican or monarchist the whole coat of arms, or indifferent to anything in public life, is it not true that *et nunc et semper et in secula* the sincere poet will see himself, will feel himself, will know himself *damned* by the rule of any faction, o Stello?

The poet furrows his brow over the public, but his eye dilates and his heart grows strong and firm without closing, and it is so that he prefaces his definitive choice of being:

CETTE NUIT

Quand l'ombre menaça de la fatale loi
Tel vieux Rêve, désir et mal de mes vertèbres,
Affligé de périr sous les plafonds funèbres
Il a ployé son aile indubitable en moi.

Luxe, ô salle d'ébène où, pour séduire un roi,
Se tordent dans leur mort des guirlandes
    célèbres,
vous n'êtes qu'un orgueil menti par les ténèbres
Aux yeux du solitaire ébloui de sa foi.

Oui, je sais qu'au lointain de cette nuit, la Terre
Jette d'un grand éclat l'insolite mystère,

Pour les siècles hideux qui l'obscurscissent moins.

L'espace à soi pareil qu'il s'accroisse ou se nie
Roule dans cet ennui des feux vils pour témoins
Que s'est d'un astre en fête allumé le génie.

THAT NIGHT

When the shadow threatened with the fatal
law such an old Dream, desire and pain of my
vertebrae, grieved with perishing under the
funereal ceilings it folded its indubitable wing in
me.

Luxury, oh ebony room where, to seduce a king,
celebrated garlands writhe in their death, you are
only a pride lied by the darkness to the eyes of the
solitary one dazzled by his faith.

Yes, I know that far off in this night, the Earth
casts with a great flash the unusual mystery, by the
hideous centuries that obscure it less.

Space like unto itself whether it grows or
negates itself flows in that boredom vile fires for
witnesses that this genius has been lit with a
festive star.

As for this sonnet, *le Tombeau d'Edgar Poe*, so beautiful is it that it seems wrong not to honor it without a sort of panicky horror,

LE TOMBEAU D'EDGAR POE

Tel qu'en Lui-même enfin l'éternité le change,
Le Poète suscite avec un glaive nu
Son siècle épouvanté de n'avoir pas connu
Que la mort triomphait dans cette voix étrange!

Eux, comme un vil sursaut d'hydre oyant jadis
    l'Ange
Donner un sens plus pur aux mots de la tribu,
Proclamèrent très haut le sortilège bu
Dans le flot sans honneur de quelque noir
    mélange.

Du sol et de la nue hostiles, ô grief!
Si notre idée avec ne sculpte un bas-relief
Dont la tombe de Poe éblouissante s'orne,

Calme bloc ici-bas chu d'un désastre obscur,
Que ce granit du moins montre à jamais sa
    borne
Aux noirs vols du Blasphème épars dans le
    futur.

Such that eternity changes Him at last into himself, the Poet provokes with a naked sword his century frightened from not having known that Death was triumphing in that strange voice!

They, like a vile recoiling of the hydra once hearing the angel give a purer meaning to the words of the tribe, proclaimed very loud the sortilege drunk from the honorless stream of some black mixture.

From the hostile ground and cloud, oh grievance! If our concept with sculpts no bas-relief to ornament the dazzling tomb of Poe,

Calm block fallen down here from an obscure disaster, may this granite at least display a milestone forever to the black flights of Blasphemy scattered in the future.

Shouldn't we end here? Does it not embody the forced abstraction of our title? Is it not, in terms rather more sibylline than lapidary, the last word on this terrible subject, at the risk of being damned as well (oh glory!) with them?

And in fact we will stop here, at this last citation which is both so representative and so intrinsically good.

It still remains for us, we know, to complete the study of Mallarmé and his work! What a pleasure that will be, however little time we are granted for this task!

Everyone (worthy of knowing it) knows that Mallarmé has published splendid editions of *L'Après-midi d'un faune*, the searing fantasy in which the Shakespeare of *Venus and Adonis* has something of the fire from the most mettlesome eclogues of Theocritus, — and the *Toast funèbre à Théophile Gautier*, noble tears shed over a true craftsman. As these poems are already in the spotlight, it seems useless for us to cite from them. Useless and impious. For that would be to destroy all of them, so unified is the definitive Mallarmé. Sooner lop off a breast from a pretty woman!

Everyone capable of appreciating such things knows equally well his beautiful linguistic studies, his *Gods of Greece* and his admirable translations of Edgar Poe.

Mallarmé now works on a book whose profundity will surprise us no less than its splendor will dazzle all but the blind, but when will this finally be, *cher ami*?

Here we stop: praise, like floods, stops at certain heights.

Besides, our goal is reached. We have glanced at the essential verses of this essential poet and it is for us, we repeat, an inutterable pride to have claimed for

Literature these invaluable names: one obscure, the other half-unknown, the third misunderstood, Tristan Corbière, Arthur Rimbaud, Stéphane Mallarmé!

In spite of two articles, one of them very thorough by the marvelous Sainte-Beuve, the other, dare we say it? rather short by Baudelaire, in spite even of a kind of good public opinion that doesn't quite assimilate her to the trend of Louise Colet, Amable Tastu, Anaïs Ségalas and other negligible bluestockings (we were forgetting Loïsa Puget, who is very entertaining for those who like that kind of thing), Marceline Desbordes-Valmore is worthy of figuring among our Cursed Poets because of her apparent but absolute obscurity, and it is our imperious obligation to speak of her at length and in as great detail as possible.

M. Barbey d'Aurevilly long ago spotted her among the ranks and signaled, with that uncanny skill of his, her strangeness and the true albeit feminine talent that she possessed.

As for us, so eager for good verse, we nevertheless did not know her, contenting ourselves with the verse of the established masters, when Arthur Rimbaud met us and practically forced us to read *all* of what we had previously thought a jumbled mess with a few beautiful patches.

Our surprise was great and needs some time to be explained.

First of all, Marceline Desbordes-Valmore was from the North and not from the South, a small difference more important than one might think. From the raw North, from the real North (the South, always cooked through, is always better, but this betterness can doubtless always be the enemy of the true Good.), — and this pleased us who are also from the raw North, at last!

So then, an utter unpretentiousness, using just the necessary words, and taking consistent pains that her work is only ever seen in a good light. Some examples of her work will attest to what we like to call our wisdom.

While awaiting these citations may we not return to the total absence of the South in this fairly considerable oeuvre? And yet how ardently understood is her Spanish North (but doesn't Spain have a phlegmatic side and a haughtiness even colder than all Britishness?), her North

Où vinrent s'asseoir les ferventes Espagnes.

Where the ardent Spains came to settle.

Yes, none of the histrionics, none of the fake jewelry, none of the deplorable bad faith found even the most indisputable masterworks from outre-Loire. And nevertheless how hot are these youthful romances, these memories from a woman's age, these maternal tremblings! So sweet, and so earnest! What landscapes, what love of the land! And this passion, so chaste, so discreet, and nevertheless so strong and moving!

We had said that the language of Marceline Desbordes-Valmore was economical, it is very adequate that it must be said; only that we are of such purists, and such pedants, let us add, given that they call us "decadents" (an insult, between parentheses, implying picturesque, autumnal, with a setting sun, to sum it up) that only certain naiveties, but no artlessness of style, could excite our writerly prejudices which thirst for the impeccable. The truth of our revaluation will shine in the course of the citations which we will now lavishly give.

But the chaste yet strong passion that we were pointing out, the almost excessive emotion we were exalting . . . it has to be said that after reading her work — which, because conscious of our first adulatory paragraphs, is bound to be uneasy — our high opinion of her remains intact.

And here is the proof:

UNE LETTRE DE FEMME

Les femmes, je le sais, ne doivent pas écrire;
    J'écris pourtant
Afin que dans mon coeur au loin tu puisses lire
    Comme en partant.

Je ne tracerai rien qui ne soit dans toi-même
    Beaucoup plus beau:
Mais le mot cent fois dit, venant de ce qu'on aime,
    Semble nouveau.

Qu'il te porte au bonheur! Moi, je reste à l'attendre,
    Bien que, là-bas,
Je sens que je m'en vais, pour voir et pour entendre
    Errer tes pas.

Ne te détourne pas s'il passe un hirondelle
    Par le chemin,
Car je crois que c'est moi qui passerai fidèle
    Toucher ta main.

Tu t'en vas: tout s'en va! tout se met en voyage,
    Lumière et fleurs;
Le bel été te suit, me laissant à l'orage,
    Lourde de pleurs.

Mais si l'on ne vit plus que d'espoir et d'alarmes,
    Cessant de voir,

Partageons pour le mieux: moi je retiens les larmes,
    Garde l'espoir.

Non, je ne voudrais pas, tant je te suis unie,
    Te voir souffrir:
Souhaiter la douleur à sa moitié bénie,
    C'est se haïr.

LETTER FROM A WOMAN

Women, I know, shouldn't write; Yet I write so
that you can read in my heart from afar as while
taking leave.

I won't write anything that isn't, in you, much
more handsome: But the word said a hundred
times, coming from the beloved, seems new.

Don't look away if a swallow should pass by the
path, for I believe that it's I who am coming by,
loyal, to touch your hand.

You go away: everything goes away! All takes
up traveling, light and flowers; the lovely summer
follows you, leaving me to the storm, heavy with
weeping.

But if one keeps living only on hope and
alarms, ceasing to see, let them advantageously:
me, I take the tears, you, keep the hope.

No, I would not like, bound as I am to you, to see you suffer: wishing pain on one's blessed other half is to hate oneself.

Is it not divine? But wait.

JOUR D'ORIENT

Ce fut un jour, pareil à ce beau jour,
Que, pour tout perdre, incendiait l'amour.

C'était un jour de charité divine
Où, dans l'air bleu, l'éternité chemine;
Où, dérobée à son poids étouffant,
La terre joue et redevient enfant.
C'était, partout, comme un baiser de mère
Long rêve errant dans une heure éphémère,
Heure d'oiseaux, de parfums, de soleil,
D'oubli de tout . . . hors du bien sans pareil!
. . . .
Ce fut un jour, pareil à ce beau jour,
Que pour tout perdre incendiait l'amour.

That was a day, similar to that fine day, that, at risk of losing all, ignited love.

It was a day of holy charity when, in the blue air, eternity walks forward; when, stripped of its stifling weight, the land frolics and becomes a child again.

It was, everywhere, like a mother's kiss long roving dream in an ephemeral hour, hours of birds, of odors, of sunlight, of forgetfulness of all . . . except the matchless good!

It was a day, like that fine day that at risk of losing all ignited love.

We must restrain ourselves, and leave room for examples from another period.

And, before moving on to examine her more austere sublimities, if it is permissible to so describe part of this adorably gentle woman's work, let us, tears literally in our eyes, recite with the pen this one:

RENONCEMENT

Pardonnez-moi, Seigneur, mon visage attristé,
Vous qui l'aviez formé de sourire et de charmes;
Mais sous le front joyeux vous aviez mis les
    larmes,
Et de vos dons, Seigneur, ce don seul m'est resté.

C'est le moins envié; c'est le meilleur peut-être:
Je n'ai plus à mourir à mes liens de fleurs.
Ils vous sont tous rendus, cher auteur de mon être,

Et je n'ai plus à moi que le sel de mes pleurs.

Les fleurs sont pour l'enfant, le sel est pour la
    femme:
Faites-en l'innocence et trempez-y mes jours.
Seigneur, quand tout ce sel aura lavé mon âme,
vous me rendrez un coeur pour vous aimer
    toujours!

Tous mes étonnements sont finis sur la terre,
Tous mes adieux sont faits, l'âme est prête à
    jaillir;
Pour atteindre à ses fruits protégés de mystère
Que la pudique mort a seule osé cueillir.

O sauveur! Soyez tendre au moins à d'autres mères,
Par amour pour la vôtre et par pitié pour nous!
Baptisez leurs enfants de nos larmes amères,
Et relevez les miens tombés à vos genoux.

RENUNCIATION

    Forgive me, Lord, my saddened face, you who
had shaped it from smile and charm, but, under
the joyful brow, you had put tears: and of your
gifts, Lord, this gift alone is left me.

It is the least envied; it is the best, perhaps. I have no more to die at my chains of flowers. They are all returned to you, dear author of my being, and I have nothing left for me but the salt of my weeping . . .

Flowers are for the child, salt is for the woman: Make innocence of it and dip my days into it. Lord, when all this salt will have washed my soul, you will give me back a heart to love you forever.

All my surprises are over on earth, all my goodbyes are made, the soul is ready to burst forth to attain its fruits protected by mystery which chaste death alone has dared to pick.

Oh Savior! Be gentle at least to other mothers out of love for your own and out of pity for us! Baptize their children with our bitter tears and lift up again mine, fallen at your knees.

How this sadness surpasses that of *Olympio* and of À *Olympio*, however beautiful (especially the latter) these two proud poems may be! But, refined readers, forgive us, on the threshold of other sanctuaries in this church of a hundred chapels which is the work of Marceline Desbordes-Valmore, — for singing along with you here:

Que mon nom ne soit rien qu'une ombre douce
    et vaine,
Qu'il ne cause jamais ni l'effroi ni la peine,
Q'un indigent l'emporte après m'avoir parlé
Et le garde longtemps dans son coeur consolé!

May my name be nothing but a soft, useless
shadow, may it never cause fear or pain, may a
pauper take it with him after talking to me and
keep it long after in his consoled heart.

Have you forgiven us?

We have said that we will try to speak of the poet in
all her aspects.

Let us proceed in order, and we are sure that you
will be satisfied by as many examples as possible. Here
also are some abusively long specimens from the young
girl, a romantic since 1820, and of a better Parny, writing in a form scarcely different, all the while remaining singularly original.

L'INQUIÉTUDE

Qu'est-ce donc qui me trouble? Et qu'est-ce qui
    m'attend?
Je suis triste à la ville et m'ennuie au village;
    Les plaisirs de mon âge

Ne peuvent me sauver de la longeur du temps.
Autrefois l'amitié, les charmes de l'étude
Remplissaient sans effort mes paisibles loisirs.
Oh! quel est donc l'objet de mes vagues désirs?
Je l'ignore et le cherche avec inquiétude.
Si, pour moi, le bonheur n'était pas la gaîté,
Je ne le trouve plus dans la mélancolie;
Mais si je crains les pleurs autant que la folie,
     Où trouver la félicité?

. . . .

DISQUIET

What is it then that troubles me? And what
awaits me? I am sad in the city and bored in the
village; the pleasures of my age cannot save me
from the lengthiness of time. In other times
friendship, the appeals of study, effortlessly filled
my peaceful leisure. Oh! What is the object of my
unclear desires? I don't know it and I look for it
with disquiet. If, for me, happiness was not the
same as gaiety, I no longer find it in melancholy;
but if I fear the weeping as much as madness,
where do I find happiness?

She next addresses her "Reason," imploring and re-
nouncing it together — and so politely. Of the rest we
admire this monologue in the style of Corneille, more
tender than Racine but proud and dignified like the
style of those two great poets, though with a very different accent.

Among a thousand rather delicate niceties, never
insipid and always surprising, we implore you to con-
sider in this quick walk-through a few isolated verses
with the intent of tempting you towards the whole:

Cache-moi ton regard plein d'âme et de tristesse
. . . .
On ressemble au Plaisir sous un chapeau de fleurs.
. . . .
Inexplicable coeur, énigme pour toi-même . . .
. . . .
Dans ma sécurité tu ne vois qu'un délire.
. . . .

. . . Trop faible esclave, écoute,
Écoute et ma raison te pardonne et t'absout.
Rends-lui du moins les pleurs! Tu vas céder sans
    doute?
Hélas non! toujours non! O mon coeur, prends
    donc tout!

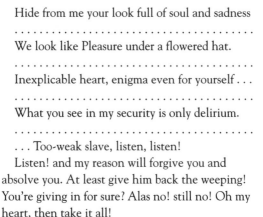

Hide from me your look full of soul and sadness

. . . .

We look like Pleasure under a flowered hat.

. . . .

Inexplicable heart, enigma even for yourself . . .

. . . .

What you see in my security is only delirium.

. . . .

. . . Too-weak slave, listen, listen!
Listen! and my reason will forgive you and
absolve you. At least give him back the weeping!
You're giving in for sure? Alas no! still no! Oh my
heart, then take it all!

As for *La Prière perdue*, from which these last lines
are taken, we made amends for our already too-repeated
word *delicacy* of which there is only one instance. With
Marceline Desbordes-Valmore, one often doesn't know
what to say or hold back, so much are you deliciously
troubled by this genius, an enchantress by herself en-
chanted.

If any poem has the articulate passion of the best
elegies, it's this one — or we don't want to hear about it.

And the affections of this tender and noble woman
are so pure, her loves so chaste that what more can be
said other than to read all her works? Listen again to

this pair of all-too-short fragments:

LES DEUX AMOURS

. . . .
C'était l'Amour. Plus folâtre que tendre,
D'un trait sans force il effleura mon coeur;
    Il fut léger comme un riant mensonge.
. . . .
Il offrit le plaisir sans parler de bonheur.
. . . .
    C'est dans tes yeux que je vis l'autre
Amour.
. . . .
    Cet entier oubli de soi-même,
    Ce besoin d'aimer pour aimer
Et que le mot aimer semble à peine exprimer.
Ton coeur seul le renferme et le mien le devine.
Je sens à tes transports, à ma fidélité,
Qu'il veut dire à la fois bonheur, éternité,
    Et que sa puissance est divine.

THE TWO LOVES

    It was love. More frisky than tender, with a
casual remark he'll brush against my heart; He
was light like a laughing lie.

. . . .

He offered pleasure without speaking of happiness.

. . . .

It's in your eyes I see the other Love.

. . . .

The entire forgetting of oneself, this need to love for love's sake and which the word love seems hardly to express. Only your heart encloses it, and mine guesses its presence. I feel by your transports, by my loyalty, that it means at once happiness, eternity, and that its power is divine.

LES DEUX AMITIÉS

Il est deux Amitiés comme il est deux Amours;
    L'une ressemble à l'imprudence:
    C'est un enfant qui rit toujours.

There are two Friendships as there are two Loves; one resembles imprudence: it's a child who's always laughing.

And all the charm divinely describes a friendship of young girls, and then . . .

. . . .
  L'autre Amitié, plus grave, plus austère,
Se donne avec lenteur, choisit avec mystère.
. . . .
Elle écarte les fleurs de peur de s'y blesser.
. . . .
Elle voit par ses yeux et marche sur ses pas.
  Elle attend et ne prévient pas.

  The other friendship, more serious, more
austere, gives itself slowly, chooses with mystery.
. . . .
  She spreads her flowers with fear of hurting
herself.
. . . .
  She sees with the other's eyes and follows the
other's footsteps.
  She waits and doesn't tell.

There's the somber note already.

Alas, we cannot avoid restricting ourselves at the
moment to finishing this study. For what inviting feats
of local color! What landscapes of Arras and Douai,
what banks of the Scarpe! How sweet, and how whole-
somely unconventional (you know what we mean)
these young Albertines, these Inès, these Ondines,

these Laly Galines, this exquisite *"mon beau pays, mon frais berceau, air pur de ma verte contrée, soyez béni, doux point de l'univers."* ["my beautiful land, my fresh cradle, pure air of my green country, be thou blessed, sweet point of the universe."]

It is necessary then to restrict ourselves to the just (or rather unjust) limits that cold logic imposes on the desired dimensions of our little book, our miserly survey of a truly great poet. But — but! — what a shame of not citing fragments like these here, written well before Lamartine shone and which resemble, we insist, the work of a chaste Parny! And, if possible, superior in a certain, tender way!

> Dieu, qu'il est tard! Quelle surprise!
> Le temps a fui comme un éclair.
>   Douze fois l'heure a frappé l'air
>   Et près de toi je suis encore assise,
> Et loin de pressentir le moment du sommeil,
> Je croyais voir encore un rayon de soleil.
> Se peut-il que déjà l'oiseau dorme au bocage?
>   Ah! pour dormir il fait si beau!
> . . . .
> Garde-toi d'éveiller notre chien endormi;
>   Il méconnaîtrait son ami
> Et de mon imprudence il instruirait ma mère.

. . . .
Écoute la raison: va-t'en, laisse ma main,
    Il est minuit . . .

God, how late it is! What a surprise! Time fled
like a lightning bolt. Twelve times the hour has
struck the air and near to you I'm still seated, and
far from sensing the moment of drowsiness, I
thought I saw a ray of sunlight. Is it possible that
the bird still sleeps in the hedgerow? Ah! It's such
lovely weather to sleep!

. . . .
Be careful not to wake our sleeping dog; he
might not recognize his friend and would let my
mother know of my imprudence.

. . . .
Listen to reason: go, let go of my hand, it's
midnight . . .

It is pure, this "laisse ma main"; it is full of love, this
"il est minuit", after this ray of sunlight which she believed to see again!

Let us leave, sighing, the young girl. The woman,
we have glimpsed her above, such a woman! The
woman-friend, oh the woman-friend! the verses on the
death of Mme de Girardin!

La mort vient de fermer le plus beaux yeux du monde.

Death has just closed the loveliest eyes in the world.

The mother!

Quand j'ai grondé mon fils, je me cache et je pleure.

When I've yelled at my son, I hide myself and I weep.

And when this son goes to boarding school, what a terrible cry!

Candeur de mon enfant, comme on va vous détruire!

Candor of my child, how they are going to destroy you!

What has been neglected the least by Marceline Desbordes-Valmore are the adorable fables, particular to her, in the style of that bitter Lafontaine and sweet Florian.

Un tout petit enfant s'en allait à l'école;

On avait dit: allez! il tâchait d'obéir.

> A very small child went off to school;
> They told him: go! and he struggled to obey.

Oh, we beg you, to underline all these delicacies, so vital, so unaffected.

> Si mon enfant m'aime,

sings "la Dormeuse," which here means "Lullaby," but how much better!

> Dieu dira lui-même:
> J'aime cet enfant qui dort.
> Qu'on lui porte un rêve d'or.

> If my child loves me, God himself will say: I
> love this sleeping child. May he be brought a
> dream of gold.

But after having realized that Marceline Desbordes-Valmore has, the first among the poets of her time, used unusual rhythms to great effect — for instance the eleven-foot line — very artistic without being too self-conscious about it, let us resume our admiration with this admirable passage:

LES SANGLOTS

Ah! L'enfer est ici! l'autre me fait moins peur.
Pourtant le purgatoire inquiète mon coeur.

On m'en a trop parlé pour que ce nom funeste
Sur un si faible coeur ne serpente et ne reste
Et quand le flot des jours me défait fleur à fleur,
Je vois le purgatoire au fond de ma pâleur.

S'ils ont dit vrai, c'esst là qu'il faut aller
    s'éteindre,
O Dieu de toute vie! avant de vous atteindre.

C'est là qu'il faut descendre, et sans lune et sans
    jour,
Sous le poids de la crainte et la croix de l'amour;

Pour entendre gémir les âmes condamnées
Sans pouvoir dire: "Allez! vous êtes
    pardonnées!";

Sans pouvoir les tarir, ô douleur des douleurs!
Sentir filtrer partout les sanglots et les pleurs;

Se heurter dans la nuit des cages cellulaires
Que nulle aube ne teint de ses prunelles claires;

Ne savoir où crier au Sauveur méconnu:

"Hélas! mon doux Sauveur, n'êtes-vous pas
  venu?"

Ah! j'ai peur d'avoir peur, d'avoir froid: je me
  cache
Comme un oiseau tombé qui tremble qu'on
  l'attache.

Je rouvre tristement mes bras au souvenir . . .
Mais c'est le purgatoire et je le sens venir.

C'est là que je m'en vais au-devant de moi-
  même,
N'osant y souhaiter rien de tout ce que j'aime.

Je n'aurais donc plus rien de charmant dans le coeur
Que le lointain écho de leur vivant bonheur.

        Ciel! où m'en irai-je
        Sans pieds pour courir?
        Ciel! où frapperai-je
        Sans clé pour ouvrir?

Sous l'arrêt éternel repoussant ma prière
Jamais plus le soleil n'atteindra ma paupière

Pour l'essuyer du monde et des tableaux affreux
Qui font baisser partout mes regards
  douloureux.

Plus de soleil! Pourquoi? Cette lumière aimée
Aux méchants de la terre est pourtant allumée;

Sur un pauvre coupable à l'échafaud conduit
Comme un doux: "viens à moi!" l'orbe
    s'épanche et luit.

Plus de feu nulle part! Plus d'oiseaux dans
    l'espace!
Plus d'Ave Maria dans la brise qui passe!

Au bord des lacs taris un roseau plus mouvant!
Plus d'air pour soutenir un atome vivant!

Ces fruits que tout ingrat sent fondre sous sa
    lèvre
Ne feront plus couler leur fraîcheur dans ma
    fièvre;

Et de mon coeur absent qui viendra m'oppresser
J'ammasserai les pleurs sans pouvoir les verser.

    Ciel! où m'en irai-je
    Sans pieds pour courir?
    Ciel! où frapperai-je
    Sans clé pour ouvrir?

Plus de ces souvenirs qui m'emplissent de
    larmes,

Si vivants que toujours je vivrais de leurs
   charmes;

Plus de famille, au soir, assise sur le seuil
Pour bénir son sommeil chantant devant
   l'aïeul;

Plus de timbre adoré dont la grâce invincible
Eût forcé le néant à devenir sensible;

Plus de livres divins comme effeuillés des cieux,
Concerts que tous mes sens écoutaient par mes
   yeux.

Ainsi n'oser mourir quand on n'ose plus vivre,
Ni chercher dans la mort un ami qui délivre!
O parents, pourquoi donc vos fleurs sur nos
   berceaux
Si le ciel a maudit l'arbre et les arbrisseaux?

> Ciel! où m'en irai-je
> Sans pieds pour courir?
> Ciel! où frapperai-je
> Sans clé pour ouvrir?

Sans le croix qui s'incline à l'âme prosternée,
Punie après la mort du malheur d'être née!

Mais quoi! dans cette mort qui se sent expirer,

Si quelque cri lointain me disait d'espérer!

Si dans ce ciel éteint quelque étoile pâlie
Envoyait sa lueur à ma mélancolie!

Sous ces arceaux tendus d'ombre et de désespoir,
Si des yeux inquiets s'allumaient pour me voir!

Oh! ce serait ma mère intrépide et bénie
Descendant réclamer sa fille assiz punie!

Oui! ce sera ma mère ayant attendri Dieu
Qui viendra me sauver de cet horrible lieu,

Et relever au vent de la jeune espérance
Son dernier fruit tombé mordu par la
    souffrance.

Je sentirai ses bras si beaux, si doux, si forts,
M'étreindre et me'enlever dans leurs puissants
    efforts;

Je sentirai couler dans mes naissantes ailes
L'air pur qui fait monter les libres hirondelles,

Et ma mère en fuyant pour ne plus revenir
M'emportera vivante à travers l'avenir!

Mais avant de quitter les mortelles campagnes
Nous irons appeler des âmes pour compagnes,

Au bout du champ funèbre où j'ai mis tant de
    fleurs,
Nous ébattre aux parfums qui sont nés de mes
    pleurs;

Et nous aurons des voix, des transports et des
    flammes
Pour crier: "Venez-vous!" à ces dolentes âmes.

"Venez-vous vers l'été qui fait tout refleurir,
Où nous allons aimer sans pleurer, sans mourir?

"Venez, venez voir Dieu! nous sommes ses
    colombes;
Jetez là vos linceuls, les cieux n'ont plus de tombes.

"Le Sépulcre est rompu par l'éternel amour:
Ma mère nous enfante à l'éternel séjour!"

    Ah! This is hell! the other one I'm less afraid
of. And yet purgatory troubles my heart.
    I've heard too much talk about it for its fateful
name not to abide, slithering, on such a weak
heart and when the waves of days undo me
blossom by blossom, I see purgatory at the end of
my pallor.
    If they spoke truly, it's there where one must go
to extinguish oneself, oh God of all life! before

attaining you.

It's there that one must go down, and without moon or daylight, under the weight of fear and the cross of love;

In order to hear the condemned souls moan without being able to say: "Go! you are forgiven!";

Without being able to stem their misery, o pain of pains! To hear the sobs and cries filtering through everywhere;

The jostling through the night of single, separate cages which no dawn will dye with its clear eyes.

Not knowing where to cry out to the hidden Savior, "Alas! my sweet Savior, have you not come?"

Ah! I'm afraid of being afraid, of being cold: I hide myself like a fallen bird that trembles, fearing being tied down.

I open my arms sadly to memory . . . but it's purgatory and I feel it come.

It's there that I go away before myself, not daring to hope there for anything that I love.

I would then have nothing delightful left in my heart other than the faraway echo of their living happiness.

Oh heavens! where will I go without feet for

running? Oh heavens! Where will I knock
without a key for opening?

Under the eternal cessation rejecting my prayer
never more will the sun reach my eyelid

To wipe away the world and the horrible scenes
which make me lower my pained gaze.

No more sun! Why? This beloved light is still
lit up for the earth's wicked;

On a poor guilty man being led to the scaffold
like a soft "come to me!" the globe spread itself
and shines.

No more fire anywhere! No more birds in the
void! No more Hail Marys in the passing breeze!

At the edge of the dried lakes no more moving
reeds! No more air to sustain a living atom!

These fruits that every ingrate feels melt under
his lips will no longer make their coolness flow in
my fever;

And in my absent heart which will come to
oppress me I'll gather up the tears without being
able to release them.

Oh heavens! where will I go without feet for
running? Oh heavens! Where will I knock
without a key for opening?

No more memories which fill me with tears, so
alive that I could still live by their delights;

No more family, at night, sitting on the doorstep, singing before grandfather to bless his sleep;

No more adored tones whose invincible grace would force the void to become sensate;

No more holy books as if cut from the heavens, concerts which all my senses listen to through my eyes.

Thus not daring to die when one doesn't dare to live, nor to search in death for a liberating friend! Oh kinfolk, why then your flowers on our cradles if the heavens have cursed the tree and the shrubs?

Oh heavens! where will I go without feet for running? Oh heavens! Where will I knock without a key for opening?

Without the cross that leans over to the prostrated spirit, punished after death with the misfortune of having been born!

But what! in this death which one feels expiring, if only some distant cry told me to hope!

If in the snuffed-out sky some pallid star sent its light to my melancholy!

Under the arches straining with loads of shadow and despair, if two worried eyes lit up to see me!

Oh! That would be my bold and blessed mother coming down to reclaim her quite punished child!

Yes! That would be my mother who, having softened God's heart, will come to save me from this awful place,

And lift to the wind of young hope her last fallen fruit bit by suffering.

I will feel her arms, so pretty, so gentle, so strong, embrace me and raise me up with her potent efforts;

I will feel in my nascent wings the flow of pure air that makes the free swallows climb

And my mother while fleeing never more to return will carry me away alive across the future!

But before leaving the mortal fields we will go to call other souls for companions,

At the end of the funereal field where I have lain so many flowers, to frolic with us in the perfumes which are born of my tears;

And we will have voices, high spirits and flames to cry: "Come ye! to these dolorous souls.

"Do you come towards the summer which makes all flower again, where we will go to love without crying, without dying?

"Come, come to see God! we are his doves;

throw off your shrouds, the heavens have no more graves.

"The Tomb is broken by eternal love: my mother gives birth to us at the eternal home!"

Here the pen falls from our hands and delicious tears moisten and blur our inky scrawling. We feel impotent to dissect such an angel!

And, as a pedant, because that is our pitiable métier, we proclaim ourselves in a loud and intelligible voice that Marceline Desbordes-Valmore is quite frankly — along with George Sand, who is so different, so hard, not without her charming indulgences, of great common sense, of proud and therefore of male allure — the only woman of genius and talent of this century, and of all centuries, in the company of Sappho perhaps, and Saint Theresa.

"One should only write for the whole world . . . "

"Besides, what does justice matter to us? He who at birth does not carry his own glory in his breast will never understand the meaning of this word."

These words, taken from the preface of *La Révolte* (1870), encapsulate all of Villiers de l'Isle-Adam, the man and the work.

Immense pride, and justified.

All of Paris — the literary and artistic Paris, the nocturnal city lingering over great discussions rather than private, gas-lit pleasures — knows him, and if it doesn't love him, then certainly respects this man and genius, perhaps not loving him enough because of the admiration he is due.

A great head of greying hair; a broad face which seems to enlarge his magnificently dreamy eyes; mustachioed with a chin-tuft; making frequent gestures, he is a thousand leagues from ugly but sometimes strange, his sometimes disconcerting conversation often jolted by a burst of hilarity, then giving way to the most mellifluous intonations in the world, a slow and calm basso, now suddenly rising to a contralto. And what eloquence, always as disturbing as possible! A terror sometimes passes through his paradoxes, a terror which seems shared by the speaker; then a mad laugh contorts both the speaker and his listeners, his speech now blazing with new wit and comic force. All the necessary opinions and nothing that might bore one are on parade in this magical current. And when Villiers goes away he leaves behind something like a black atmosphere which stays in the eyes, like the simultaneous memory of pyrotechnics, a burning building, lightning flashes, and the sun!

The work is much harder to describe, and to get hold of, than the man who made it, whom one often meets. The work is exceedingly difficult to find. We mean almost impossible, because this gentleman poet, owing to his disdain for noise and his lofty indolence, has neglected banal publicity in favor of his true and only glory.

He begins with superb verse as a child. But try and find them! Go look for *Morgane*, *Elën*, these dramas as few among the greatest dramatists have made; go search for *Claire Lenoir*, one of this century's unique novels! And then, in the end there is *Axel* and *L'Ève future*, these pure masterpieces interrupted over the years, but always resumed, like cathedrals and revolutions.

Happily, Villiers promises us a full edition of his complete works, in six volumes, to come very soon.

Although Villiers may already be VERY GLORIOUS,

and his name may be destined to be deeply held by an endless posterity, nevertheless we class him among the *Damned Poets*, BECAUSE HE HAS NOT BEEN GLORIFIED ENOUGH in these times which should be at his feet.

And wait! For us as for many *bons esprits*, l'Académie Française — which has given to Leconte de l'Isle the chair of the renowned Hugo, who was, to speak frankly, one manner of great poet — has good members and better members, and given that the Immortals of the Pont des Arts have at last consecrated the tradition of a great poet replacing a great poet ever since the considerable poet who was Népomucène Lemercier replaced . . . we don't remember whom. Who could take his place after death, which we hope to be far away, this Classical and Barbaric poet, if not Monsieur le Comte de Villiers de l'Isle-Adam, recommended by his enormous title of nobility, and above all by his immense talent, the fantastic genius of this charming comrade, this accomplished man of the world without any of the corresponding flaws; who, if not Villiers de l'Isle-Adam?

Now we extract some passages, namely, the "silent scene" of *La Révolte*.

The clock above the door sounds the morning hour, somber music; then, between fairly long silences, two o'clock, then half past two, then three o'clock, then half past three, then finally four o'clock. Félix remains passed out. The early daylight begins to cross the windowpanes, the candles go out; a candle-holder shatters by itself, the fire pales.

The door at the end slams open; enter Mme Élisabeth trembling, frightfully pale; she holds her handkerchief over her mouth. Without seeing her husband, she goes slowly to the great armchair, by the fireplace. She throws off her hat, and with her forehead in her hands, eyes transfixed, she sits and begins to dream aloud in a soft voice, — She is cold; her teeth chatter and she shivers.

and the tenth scene of the third act of *Nouveau Monde* in which, after the very spiritual and eloquent exposé of the financial and land-owning grievances of the English tenant farmers in America, everyone speaks at the same time, as two brackets indicate, — and as shown here with the brackets reduced to the proportions of our text.

⌈ EFFIE, NOELLA, MAUD *intoning a psalm:* ⌉
 ⌊ "Super flumina Babylonis . . ." ⌋

OFFICER *behind Tom Burnett seated on a stool and with a bawling volubility, overriding the psalm:* You're late, Sir Tom! It's the day of return. You're positively late. You've signed more treaties with the German explorers: it costs 63 thalers which they pronounce dollars . . . *(Birdsong in the foliage.)*

EFFIE, MAUD, NOELLA, *louder.* "Sedimus et flebimus . . ."

OFFICER *shouting in Tom Burnett's ear.* . . . And with the merchants of Philadelphia! There are strong rights to perceive as well. As for the industrial operations, here's the invoice . . .

LE CHÉROKÉE *seated on his barrel.* Drink the wine! Drink it down! The sap of the flowering maple!

QUAKER EADIE *reading aloud.* The birds awake at noon. They start their hymns again and all in nature . . .

(The hound barks)

LIEUTENANT HARRIS, *showing Tom Burnett.* Silence! Let him speak.

A REDSKIN *confidentially to a group of blacks.* If you see the bees, the white men are coming; if you see the bison the Indian follows them.

MR. O'KEENE, *to a group of people.*

They say that frightful things have happened in Boston. Just listen . . .

TOM BURNETT, *beside himself with anger, to the officer*

Late! but that's my ruin! Where will this ever end? Tax the air that I breathe! Why do you not stop me in the corner of the woods, all of a sudden? Have I not lived to see that? That's the point of traveling, to become an honest man! Absolutely, I like the Mohawks better.

(Furious, towards the women:)

Oh! that psalm!

Monkeys swing by on vines.

A COMANCHE, *apart, looking at them.*

Why did the Man On High place the red man at the center and the whites all around?

MAUD, *all in one breath, the eyes to the sky and showing Tom Burnett . . .*

What eloquence the great spirit lends him!

This ensemble should last no longer than half a minute. It is one of those moments of confusion when the crowd itself speaks.

It is a sudden explosion of tumult where one can only distinguish the words "dollars," "psalms," "Late!" "Babylonis," "Let him speak," etc., mixed with barking, the cries of children, the squawking of

> *parrots. — Frightened monkeys leap from the*
> *branches, birds cross the theater from one side to*
> *the other.*

These two scenes have been bitterly criticized, even scoffed at, which only underlines the correspondence of our title to our subject.

And here people have been wrong, for it must be understood that Theater, that *relatively* conventional medium, must make concessions to the modern poet which it could not allowably grant our ancestors.

Let us explain.

It is neither Shakespeare, with his sign-post stage directions, nor the Spanish theater with its *jornadas* that can contain years and years of which we speak.

No, it is to the scrupulous Father Corneille, to the tender and no less correct Racine, and to the no less correct if hardly tender Molière that Villiers returns. The unity of place, sometimes broken by Molière, is matched in all three by an equally violated unity of time. Now, what has Villiers wanted to do in the two scenes just offered, if not profit, in the first, from all that the stage allowed the three French Classics, when their plots run into situations that are too strict for the constricting twenty-four hours prescribed Aristotle, — in the second, from the same tolerance which they have not dared to use, it is true, for that which concerns a state of things faster in some way than the spoken word, tolerance that music exploits every day with duos, trios *et tutti*, and Painting with perspective.

But no, the contemporary genius is forbidden to do what the genius of antiquity did. People have laughed a lot over the SILENT SCENE and over the SCENE IN WHICH EVERYONE SPEAKS, and they will keep laughing for a long time. Meanwhile, we have just irrefutably proved to you (and there is no doubt that you agree) that Villiers not only had the right, but was also thoroughly justified in writing these scenes as he would have been a thousand times wrong not to write them. *Durus rex, sed Rex.*

The work of Villiers, we remember, will be published some day, and we forcefully hope that success — you understand? — SUCCESS will lift the curse that weighs on this admirable poet whom we would regret to leave so soon, if it were not a chance to send him our most cordial: *Courage!*

We will not speak of the *Contes cruels*, because that particular book has already cut its swathe. There one finds, among miraculous novellas, some all-too rare verses from the poet's maturity, very short, bittersweet poems addressing or made à propos some woman, probably loved formerly and surely despised today — as so often seems to happen. We will display a few short extracts.

RÉVEIL

O toi dont je reste interdit,
J'ai donc le mot de ton abîme.
. . . .
Sois oubliée en tes hivers!

AWAKENING

Oh you from whom I remain forbidden, I have the word from your inner depths.
. . . .
May you be forgotten in your winters!

ADIEU

Un vertige épars sous tes voiles
Tenta mon front vers tes bras nus.
. . . .
Et tes cheveux couleur de deuil
Ne font plus d'ombre sur mes rêves

FAREWELL

A scattered dizziness under your veils tempted my brow to your bare arms.

. . . .

And your hair the color of mourning cast no more shadow on my dreams.

RENCONTRE

Tu secouais ton noir flambeau,
Tu ne pensais pas être morte:
J'ai forgé la grille et la porte
Et mon coeur est sûr du tombeau!

. . . .

Tu ne ressusciteras pas!

ENCOUNTER

You were waving your black torch, you didn't think you were dead: I forged the iron grate and the door and my heart is certain of the grave!

. . . .

You will not rise again!

And how to restrain ourselves from bestowing you

this time with a poem in its entirety? As in *Isis*, as in *Morgane*, as in *Nouveau Monde*, as in all his works, Villiers evokes here the specter of a mysterious woman, a haughty queen, somber and proud like the night, always crepuscular with shimmers of blood and gold on her soul and her beauty.

AU BORD DE LA MER

Au sortir de ce bal nous suivîmes les grèves;
Vers le toit d'un exil, au hasard du chemin,
Nous allions: une fleur se fanait dans sa main;
C'était par un minuit d'étoiles et de rêves.

Dans l'ombre, autour de nous, tombaient des
    flots foncés.
Vers les lointains d'opale et d'or, sur
    l'Atlantique,
L'outre-mer épandait sa lumière mystique,
Les algues parfumaient les espaces glacés.

Les vieux échos sonnaient dans la falaise
    entière!
Et les nappes de l'onde aux volutes sans frein
Écumaient, lourdement, contre les rocs
    d'airain.
Sur la dune brillaient les croix d'un cimetière.

Leur silence, pour nous, couvrait ce vaste bruit.
Elles ne tendaient plus, croix par l'ombre
    insultées,
Les couronnes de deuil, fleurs de mort,
    emportées
Dans les flots tonnants, par les tempêtes, la
    nuit.

Mais de ces blancs tombeaux en pente sur la
    rive,
Sous la brume sacrée à des clartés pareils,
L'ombre questionnait en vain les grands
    sommeils:
Ils gardaient le secret de la Loi décisive.

Frileuse, elle voilait d'un cachemire noir,
Son sein, royal exil de toutes mes pensées!
J'admirais cette femme aux paupières baissées,
Sphinx cruel, mauvais rêve, ancien désespoir!

Ses regards font mourir les enfants. Elle passe
Et se laisse survivre en ce qu'elle détruit.
C'est la femme qu'on aime à cause de la Nuit,
Et ceux qu'elle a connus en parlent à voix
    basse.

Le danger la revêt d'un rayon familier:

Même dans son étreinte oublieusement tendre,
Ses crimes, évoqués, sont tels qu'on croit
    entendre
Des crosses de fusils tombant sur le palier.

Cependant, sous la honte illustre qui
    l'enchaîne,
Sous le deuil où se plaît cette âme sans essor
Repose une candeur inviolée encor
Comme un lys enfermé dans un coffret d'ébène.

Elle prêta l'oreille au tumulte des mers,
Inclina son beau front touché par les années,
Et se remémorant ses mornes destinées,
Elle se répandit en ces termes amers:

"Autrefois, autrefois, — quand je faisais partie
Des vivants, — leurs amours sous les pâles
    flambeaux
Des nuits, comme la mer au pied de ces
    tombeaux,
Se lamentaient, houleux, devant mon apathie.

"J'ai vu de longs adieux sur mes mains se briser:
Mortelle, j'accueillais, sans désir et sans haine,
Les aveux suppliants de ces âmes en peine:
Le sépulcre à la mer ne rend pas son baiser.

"Je suis donc insensible et faite de silence
Et je n'ai pas vécu; mes jours sont froids et
    vains:
Les Cieux m'ont refusé les battements divins!
On a faussée pour moi les poids de la balance.

"Je sens que c'est mon sort même dans le trépas:
Et, soucieux encor des regrets ou des fêtes,
Si les morts vont chercher leurs fleurs dans les
    tempêtes,
Moi je reposerai, ne les comprenant pas."

Je saluai les croix lumineuses et pâles.
L'étendue annonçait l'aurore, et je me pris
A dire, pour calmer ses ténébreux esprits
Que le vent des remords battait de ses rafales

Et pendant que la mer déserte se gonflait:
— "Au bal vous n'aviez pas de ces mélancolies
Et les sons de cristal de vos phrases polies
Charmaient le serpent d'or de votre bracelet.

Rieuse et respirant une touffe de roses,
Sous vos grands cheveux noirs mêlés de
    diamants,
Quand la valse nous prit, tous deux, quelques
    moments,

Vous eûtes, en vos yeux, des lueurs moins
    moroses.

J'étais heureux de voir sous le plaisir vermeil
Se ranimer votre âme à l'oubli toute prête,
Et s'éclairer enfin votre douleur distraite
Comme un glacier frappé d'un rayon de soleil."

Elle laissa briller sur moi ses yeux funèbres
Et la pâleur des morts ornait ses traits fatals.
— "Selon vous, je ressemble aux pays boréals,
J'ai six mois de clartés et six mois de ténèbres?

Sache mieux quel orgueil nous nous sommes
    donnés!
Et tout ce qu'en nos yeux il empêche de lire . . .
Aime-moi, toi qui sais que, sous un clair
    sourire,
Je suis pareille à ces tombeaux abandonnés."

AT THE SEASIDE

   Leaving the ball we followed the shores;
towards the roof of an exile, not knowing where
the path led, we were going along: a flower
withered in her hand; it was during a midnight of
stars and dreams.

In the shadow, around us, fell dark streams. In the distances of gold and opal, on the Atlantic, the overseas lands were spreading their mystical light, the algaes scenting the frozen spaces.

The old echoes sounded on the entire cliff! And the wave's sheets with unbridled volutes were foaming, heavily, against the bronze rocks. On the dune shone the crosses of a cemetery.

Their silence, for us, covered this vast noise. They were no longer offering, crosses insulted by the shadows, the wreathes of mourning, flowers of death, carried away by the thundering waves, by the storms, at night.

But to these white tombs on the bank's slope, like bright spots under the sacred fog, the shadow questioned their great slumbers in vain: they kept the secret of the decisive Law.

Feeling the cold, she covered with black cashmere her breast, royal exile of all my thoughts! I admired this woman with lowered eyelids, cruel sphinx, bad dream, ancient despair!

Her gaze makes the children die. She passes and can only survive in what she destroys. She is the woman one loves because of the Night, and those whom she has known speak of her in a lowered voice.

Danger dresses her in a familiar ray: even in her forgetfully tender embrace, her crimes, when recalled, are such that one believes to hear rifle butts falling on the stair landing.

Meanwhile, under the celebrated shame that enchains her, under the mourning where that flightless soul pleases itself rests a still inviolate innocence like a lily enclosed in an ebony casket.

She lent her ear to the seas' tumult, leaned her lovely brow touched by the years, and calling her dark destinies to mind, she held forth in these bitter terms:

"Long ago, long ago, — when I was among the living, — their loves under the pale torches of the nights, like the sea at the foot of these graves, lamented themselves, howling, before my apathy.

"I have seen long goodbyes shatter on my hands: A mortal, I received without desire and without hate, the pleading vows of these lost souls: The grave does not return the sea's kiss.

"I am insensitive then and made of silence and I have not lived; my days are cold and useless: The Heavens have refused me the holy pulsations! They have falsified the balance's weights for me.

"I feel that it's my fate even in death: And, still

mindful of their regrets or of festing, if the dead go
to search for their flowers in the storms, me, I will
rest, not understanding them."

I greeted the pale and luminous crosses. The
expanse of sea announced the dawn, and I caught
myself saying to calm her dark spirits that the
wind of remorse beat with its squalls

And while the desert sea swelled up: "At the
ball you had none of this melancholia and the
crystal sounds of your polished utterances
charmed the golden serpent of your bracelet.

"Laughing and breathing a bunch of roses,
under your long black hair mixed with diamonds,
when the waltz took us, both, for a few moments,
you had, in your eyes, a glow less morose.

"I was happy to see under the bright red
pleasure your soul revive, ready for oblivion, and
clear up at last your residual pain like a glacier
struck by a ray of sunlight."

She let her gloomy eyes shine on me and the
pallor of the dead adorned her deathly features.
"According to you, I resemble the boreal lands, I
have six months of brightness and six months of
darkness?

"Be aware the pride we have given ourself! And
all that in our eyes which it keeps us from

reading . . . Love me, you who know that, behind
a bright smile, I am like these abandoned graves."

And, in these verses which one must call sublime,
we will definitively take leave — so damned little
space! — of the friend who made them.

This Damned One might well have had the most melancholy destiny, because these two mild words can, in sum, characterize the sadness of his existence, owing to his lack of guile and the perhaps irremediable indolence of heart which made him once say to himself, of himself, in his book *Sapientia*,

> Et puis, surtout, ne va pas t'oublier toi-même,
> Traînassant ta faiblesse et ta simplicité
> partout ou l'on bataille et partout ou l'on aime,
> D'une façon si triste et folle en vérité!
> . . . .
> A-t-on assez puni cette lourde innocence?

And so, above all, don't go and forget yourself, dragging your weakness and naiveté everywhere they fight and everywhere they love, in a way that is, in truth, so sad and crazy!

. . . .

Hasn't this weighty innocence been punished enough?

And in his volume *Charité*, which has just come out:

J'ai la fureur d'aimer, mon coeur si faible est fou.

. . . .

Je ne puis plus compter les chutes de mon
    coeur.

I have the furor of loving, my heart is so weak
and crazed.

. . . .

I can no longer count my heart's steep falls.

and which were the only elements, understand this
well, of that storm which is his life!

He had a happy childhood.

His parents were exceptional: a first-rate father, a
charming mother, both dead, alas! who spoiled him
like the only child he was. All the same, he was sent
to boarding school at a young age and there begins his
ruin. We can still picture him in his long black shirt,
his hair closely cropped, his fingers in his mouth, lean-
ing against the barrier between two playgrounds, crying almost in the middle of the other children, who,
already hardened, were busy at play. That very night
he ran away from school but was taken back the next
day, by means of sweetmeats and promises, where later
he "abused himself," became a young tough but not
too naughty with a lot of daydreaming in his head. He

136

was an indifferent student, and after some mixed aca-
demic success he passed his baccalaureate, this in spite
of the laziness which, we repeat, was no more than
daydreaming. Posterity will know, if it concerns itself
with him, that the lycées Bonaparte, Condorcet,
Fontanes, then Condorcet again were the establish-
ments where he wore out the britch-ends of his adolescence. A semester or two at law school and a
passable amount of draught beer drunk in the dive bars
of this epoch completed his mediocre study of the classics, all to a sketchy backdrop of brasseries and fast
women. It is from this moment that he dedicated himself to verse. Already, since he was fourteen, he had
been rhyming himself half to death, writing some
really rather droll poems in the obsceno-macabre
genre. Very quickly he burnt, but forgot still faster,
these shapeless but amusing efforts and published
Mauvaise Étoile, shortly after several pieces which were
taken by the first *Parnasse* at Lemerre. This collec-
tion — we speak of *Mauvaise Étoile* — had a fine *succès
d'hostilité* in the press. But what did this do to Pauvre
Lelian's affinity for poetry, which was a real affinity, if
not quite a talent leaping off the page? One year later
he published *Pour Cythère*, where very serious progress
was made by the Critics. This little book even caused
a stir in the world of poets. One year later, a new book-

let, *Corbeille de noces* [Wedding Baskets] proclaimed the sweetness and grace of his fiancée . . . . And it is from here that we can date "his wound."

At the end of this deadly period *Sapientia* came out, already cited above. Four years before, in the midst of a whirlwind, it had been the turn of *Flûte et Cor* [Flute and Horn], a volume of which we have since spoken much, for it contained many rather novel items.

The conversion of Pauvre Lelian to Catholicism was preceded by *Sapientia*, and the subsequent publication of a rather eclectic culling, *Avant-hier et hier*, in which less austere tones alternated with poems that were almost too mystical, made a polite but lively poetic explosion in the small world of true Letters.

Wasn't a poet free to make anything, provided it was beautiful and well-made? Or did he have to immure himself in one genre, under the pretext of unity? Asked by many of his friends about this subject, our author, whatever his native horror of these kinds of consultations, responded with a rather long digression, not without interest for its naiveté, which our readers will perhaps examine.

Here is that piece:

"Like every artist, it is certain that the poet, after acquiring intensity, that indispensable heroic condition, should then search for unity. Unity of tone (which

138

is not monotony), a recognizable style at any place in his work taken at random, some habits, a few attitudes, unity of thought as well — it is here that a debate can take place. Instead of using abstractions, we are going quite simply to take our poet himself as a field of disputation. His work beginning in 1880 bifurcates into two very distinct paths and the prospectus of his future books indicates that he has decided to continue this system of publishing, if not simultaneously (besides, this only depends on circumstantial conveniences and is outside our discussion), then at least in a parallel fashion, putting out works of an absolute difference of ideas — to be more precise, those books in which Catholicism unfolds its logic and its charms, its blandishments and its terrors; and other, purely worldly books: sensual with a distressing good humor and full of pride in life. What should become of the recommended unity of thought in all this?

"But it is there already! It is there by virtue of being human, by being Catholic, which in our eyes is the same thing. I believe, and I sin by thought as by action; I believe, and I repent by thought while waiting for better things. Or rather, I believe, and am a good Christian in that moment; I believe, and am a bad Christian in the next. Memory, hope, and the invocation of a sin delight me with or without remorse, sometimes under the same form and furnished with all the consequences of Sin; more often, both the flesh and blood are strong, — natural and animal, like the memories, hopes and invocations of the first excellent free-thinker. It pleases us — me, you, that person there, writers in general — to put this delight on paper and publish it more or less well-expressed; we consign it finally to literary form, forgetting all religious ideas — or not losing a single one from sight. Will we be, in good faith, condemned as a poet? A hundred times no. And whether the Catholic's conscience reasons thusly or not, that does not concern us.

"Now, can the Catholic verse of Pauvre Lelian be included with his other verse? A hundred times yes. The tone is always the same in the two cases, plain and solemn here, there flowery, languid, enervated, laughing and more; but the same tone everywhere, as the mystical and sensual MAN remains the intellectual man in the most varied manifestations of the same thought which its crests and troughs. And Pauvre Lelian finds himself very free to make volumes of pure prayer at the same time as volumes of pure impressions, even if the contrary might be more permissible"
. . . .

Afterwards, Pauvre Lelian produced a short book of criticism, — or rather, of exaltation — about a few

140

unrecognized poets. This little book was called *The Misunderstood*; people no longer read (among others) the work of Arthur Rimbaud, which Lelian had used to symbolize certain phases of his own destiny:

LE COEUR VOLÉ

Mon triste coeur bave à la poupe,
Mon coeur couvert de caporal:
Ils y lancent des jets de soupe,
Mon triste coeur bave à la poupe:
Sous les quolibets de la troupe
Qui pousse un rire général,
Mon triste coeur bave à la poupe,
Mon coeur couvert de caporal!

Ithyphalliques et pioupiesques,
Leurs quolibets l'ont dépravé!
Au gouvernail on voit des fresques
Ithyphalliques et pioupiesques.
Ô flots abracadabrantesques,
Prenez mon coeur, qu'il soit lavé!
Ithyphalliques et pioupiesques,
Leurs quolibets l'ont dépravé!

Quand ils auront tari leurs chiques,
Comment agir, ô coeur volé?

Ce seront des hoquets bachiques:
Quand ils auront tari leurs chiques:
J'aurai des sursauts stomachiques,
Moi, si mon coeur est ravalé:
Quand ils auront tari leurs chiques
Comment agir, ô coeur volé?

THE STOLEN HEART

My sad heart drools over the stern, my heart
covered with shag tobacco: they shoot streams of
soup at it, my sad heart drools over the stern:
under the gang's taunts which get a big laugh, my
sad heart drools over the stern, my heart covered
with shag tobacco!

Ithyphallic and barrack-room, their taunts have
debauched it! At the helm you see ithyphallic and
barrack-room frescoes. Oh abracadabrantic waves,
take my heart, may it be cleansed! Ithyphallic and
barrack-room, their taunts have debauched it!

When they have chewed up their tobacco-
plugs, what shall we do, O stolen heart? There
will be bacchic hiccups when they have chewed
up their tobacco-plugs: I'll have a heaving
stomach, me, if my heart is choked back again:

When they have chewed up their tobacco-plugs
what shall we do, O stolen heart?

TÊTE DE FAUNE

Dans la feuillée, écrin vert taché d'or,
Dans la feuillée incertaine et fleurie
De fleurs splendides où le baiser dort,
Vif et crevant l'exquise broderie,

Un faune effaré montre ses deux yeux
Et mord les fleurs rouges de ses dents blanches.
Brunie et sanglante ainsi qu'un vin vieux,
Sa lèvre éclate en rires sous les branches.

Et quand il a fui — tel qu'un écureuil —
Son rire tremble encore à chaque feuille,
Et l'on voit épeuré par un bouvreuil
Le Baiser d'or du Bois, qui se recueille.

FAUN'S HEAD

In the foliage, a green jewel-case flecked with
gold, in the uncertain foliage blossoming with
splendid flowers where the kiss sleeps, lively and
bursting through the rich embroidery,

A startled faun shows his two eyes and bites the

143

red flowers with his white teeth. Tanned and
blood-red like old wine, his lips explode in
laughter under the branches.

And when he has run away — just like a
squirrel — his laughter still quivers on each leaf,
and you can see, startled by a bullfinch, the
Golden Kiss of the Woods, which meditates.

He is currently writing, despite problems of all sorts,
several volumes. *Charité* appeared last March. *A côté*
will appear soon. The former, related to *Sapientia*, is a
volume of Catholicism both harsh and mild; the other,
a harvest of poems expressing sensations more sincere,
and more daring.

Finally, he has seen the printing of two prose works,
the *Commentaries of Socrates*, a slightly generalized
autobiography, and *Clovis Lobscure*, principal title of
many novellas of which one or two may be continued,
if God wills it.

He has many other projects. Only, he is sick and a
little discouraged, and begs your permission to go to
bed.

— Ah! later, revived, he will write and is going to
— or wants to (the same thing) — live in blessed
Beatitudo.

AVANT-PROPOS

Page 12: *Reys netos* Spanish for "Great Kings".

CORBIÈRE

Page 13: *aes triplex* Latin meaning literally "three times the money." In other words, "on the money."

Page 14: *Kriss* A kriss is a Malay dagger with a ridged and curving blade.

Page 21: *Pardon de sainte Anne* Saint Anne is the mother of the virgin Mary.

Page 21: *franc-Breton* This is a pun — a *franc-breton* is a one-franc coin while a *franc Breton* is a frank, freely forthright Breton.

RIMBAUD

Page 30: *triolet* A type of rondeau in which the first verse is repeated at the end of the first quatrain and the first two verses are repeated at the end of the second quatrain.

Page 40: *Naturalists* Naturalism was a literary trend which explored with unprecedented realism the role of social environments in determining character, motive and fate. The most famous of all the naturalists was Émile Zola.

Page 43: *Goya and Murillo* Verlaine is referring to Goya's phantasmagoric etching series *Los Caprichos*.

Page 57: *Parny* Évariste Désiré de Forges, vicomte de Parny (1753–1814). Parny was famous for his *Poésies érotiques*, which were not erotic in our sense of the word so much as amatory; also the author of *Chansons madécasses*.

Page 57: *Michelet* Jules Michelet (1798-1874), whose great history of the French Revolution belongs equally to literature as to historiography, also wrote the misogynist *L'Amour* and *La Femme*.

Page 59: *Les Veilleurs, Accroupissements, Les Pauvres à l'église, Douaniers, Les Mains de Jeanne-Marie* and *Les Soeurs de Charité* have all been recovered.

Page 60: *felix culpa* Latin for "happy fault," this is the Christian theological concept of mankind's happy fall from edenic grace, which allowed its redemption through Christ.

Page 61: *Les Illuminations* This series of prose poems has of course also been recovered.

MALLARMÉ

Page 64: *Barbey d'Aurevilly* Jules-Amédée Barbey d'Aurevilly (1808-1889), novelist (among them *Les Diaboliques* and *L'Ensorcelée*), playwright and journalist. A dandy, reactionary Catholic, renowned woman-

146

izer and high-liver, this forerunner of Decadence championed Baudelaire, Bloy and Huysmans and polemicized against not only the Parnassians but Zola and Hugo as well.

Page 64: *the Parnassians* This was a loose-knit movement of poets who aspired to a formally perfect, depersonalized poetry, as opposed to the impassioned effusions of the Romantics. So-called because of the 1867 verse anthology *Le Parnasse Contemporain*, which included works by Gautier, Baudelaire, Mallarmé, Verlaine, Cros, de Banville and others.

Page 65: *Hébé* According to Mallarmé's *Les dieux antiques*, Hebe is the Greek goddess of youth, corresponding to the Roman Juventas.

Page 72: *rebec* A bowed, usually three-stringed instrument with a pear-shaped body and a long neck, played in antiquity.

Page 75: *mandore* In English, mandola; a 16th-17th century lute that is an ancestor of the smaller mandolin.

Page 77: *Idumée* In English, Edom; the land of the descendants of Esau (son of Isaac who was disinherited in favor of Jacob). According to legend, the kings of Edom were sexless and reproduced without intercourse.

Page 81: *Edgar Poe* Edgar Allan Poe was an enormous influence on and role model for Baudelaire and his followers, especially Mallarmé, who translated Poe's verse.

DESBORDES-VALMORE

Page 87: *outre-Loire* The Loire is the unofficial boundary between northern and southern France.

Page 94: *Parny* Évariste Désiré de Forges, vicomte de Parny (1753–1814). Parny was famous for his *Poésies érotiques*, which were not erotic in our sense of the word so much as amatory; also the author of *Chansons madécasses*.

Page 100: *Arras, Douai, the Scarpe* Arras and Douai are two small cities in northern France, southwest and due south, respectively, of Lille. The Scarpe flows through both Arras and Douai.

Page 100: *Albertine, Inès, Ondine* Albertine Gantier was a childhood friend of the poet who died when she was thirty-two; she is the subject of a series of poems. Inès was the poet's firstborn daughter who died of consumption at the age of twenty-one; at her bedside Desborde-Valmore wrote "Rêve intermittent d'une nuit triste" which revisit's Inès' childhood. Ondine was the poet's second daughter, who lost her own only child at the age of four months and died herself at thirty.

Page 101: *Lamartine* Alphonse Lamartine (1790-1869) is the first Romantic poet in France, best known for the mellifluous nature poetry of his *Méditations poétiques* (1820).

Page 115: *George Sand* George Sand (1804-1876) was the pen name of Amandine Lucie Aurore Dupin, baronne Dudevant, a Romantic novelist, bohemian socialite, liberal political advocate and proto-feminist.

DE L'ISLE-ADAM

Page 116: *La Révolte* Villiers wrote the haughty and violent preface to La Révolte after the play had already opened in 1870, running for only five performances — a complete flop. However, the play was later taken up by the Symbolists — not least because of this essay — and eventually entered the repertoire of the Comédie Française. Unlike the far-out romanticism of Villiers' earlier plays Elën and Morgane, La Révolte conforms superficially to the realist bourgeois theater of its time, but only superficially: this domestic drama was shocking, disconcerting, and unmistakably anti-bourgeois.

Page 119: *Le Nouveau Monde* was Villiers' entry into an 1875 playwrighting contest to celebrate the next year's centennial of the United States' independence. The jury (which included Victor Hugo) gave no first prize but awarded two second prizes, one of them to this play. Villiers couldn't find a theater company to produce it until 1880, when it ran for twelve performances — like *La Révolte*, a dismal commercial failure.

Page 122: *jornadas* A Jornada is Spanish for journée, meaning the length of a day; this refers to Aristotle's prescription that the action represented in a drama should take no longer than a day to transpire.

Page 123: *durus rex, sed rex* "A harsh king, but the king nonetheless." Verlaine's play on words; the Latin saying is Dura lex, sed lex — "A harsh law, but the law nonetheless."

Page 123: *Contes cruels* The *Contes cruels* (Cruel Tales), published in 1883, are a hodgepodge of twenty-eight short stories written over fifteen years, ranging from scenes of Parisian life to exotic Oriental tales to pseudo-scientific fantasies to prose poems.

PAUVRE LELIAN

Page 138: *Corbeilles de noces* This phrase — meaning literally "Wedding baskets" — is a polite way of saying "dowry."

Page 144: *Beatitudo* Blessedness.

GREEN INTEGER
Pataphysics and Pedantry

Douglas Messerli, *Publisher*

Essays, Manifestos, Statements, Speeches, Maxims,
Epistles, Diaristic Notes, Narratives, Natural Histories,
Poems, Plays, Performances, Ramblings, Revelations
and all such ephemera as may appear necessary
to bring society into a slight tremolo of confusion
and fright at least.

*

GREEN INTEGER BOOKS

Green Integer EL-E-PHANT Books (6 x 9 format)